Erasmus, 1520 *(Albrecht Dürer)*

LUTHER, ERASMUS
and the REFORMATION

LUTHER, ERASMUS
and the REFORMATION

A Catholic-Protestant Reappraisal

edited by

John C. Olin

James D. Smart

Robert E. McNally, S.J.

FORDHAM UNIVERSITY PRESS

New York

CONTENTS

THE CONTRIBUTORS

ROLAND H. BAINTON — Titus Street Professor of Ecclesiastical History Emeritus, Yale University

ROBERT E. MCNALLY, S.J. — Professor of Historical Theology, Fordham University

WILHELM PAUCK — Distinguished Professor of Church History, Vanderbilt University

JOHN T. MCDONOUGH — Author of *The Law and the Gospel in Luther* (Oxford, 1963)

HAJO HOLBORN — Sterling Professor of History, Yale University

HAROLD J. GRIMM — Professor of History, Ohio State University

MARGARET MANN PHILLIPS — Author of *Erasmus and the Northern Renaissance* (London, 1949; New York, 1965) and *The Adages of Erasmus* (Cambridge, 1964)

JOHN C. OLIN — Professor of History, Fordham University

LEWIS W. SPITZ — Professor of History, Stanford University

Editorial Committee

JOHN C. OLIN — Fordham University

JAMES D. SMART — Union Theological Seminary

ROBERT E. MCNALLY, S.J. — Fordham University

PREFACE

FOUR hundred and fifty years ago, the outraged conscience of a
Christian monk shattered the peace of Christendom and initiated the
modern age. Much that we cherish in our world today was the
ultimate result of that confrontation; much that we deplore. Yet all
of our present traditions, be they Protestant, Catholic, or secular,
owe much to the turbulent ideals and struggles of the Reformation of
the sixteenth century. Both ecumenism and an undogmatic striving
for a clearer historical understanding have led scholars in increasing
numbers to re-examine, and to reassess those struggles, and the last
decade has seen a growing number of published books, papers, and
scholarly articles, all of which have shed new light on aspects of religious reform. Indeed, research is, in this fast-moving area, ahead
not only of the general impressions of the laymen, but often of the
somewhat outdated knowledge of scholars who are in neighboring
or related fields. Finally, Reformation research has for a long time
been carried on within confessional lines, and many of the best men
in the field had until recently relatively little contact with their
colleagues of another faith.

Scholars at Union Theological Seminary and Fordham University
felt that the 450th anniversary of the appearance of Luther's Ninety-
Five Theses was high time to bring Catholic and Protestant historians together to promote better understanding of the nature of the
Reformation. With the generous support of the Danforth Foundation of St. Louis, they organized a conference of leading Reformation experts, held at both Union and Fordham on October 20–21,
1967. Efforts were made not only to invite major scholars as speakers
and commentators, but to invite younger professors and graduate
students planning to study in this field. Many colleagues from related
areas of history, the social sciences, and theology were also invited,
with the aim of disseminating the content of the principal addresses,

vii

and encouraging cross-disciplinary contacts in the informal recep-
tions and meals held between formal conference sessions.

According to the *New York Times* account, about five hundred
persons attended the Fordham sessions, while those at Union, with
a more restricted seating capacity, were about half that number. It
was a lively time; the corridors were full of introductions, reunions,
and ideas. Many new friendships formed were renewed later in the
year at historical meetings in Toronto and elsewhere.

The sponsors of the conference felt that its extension through the
printed word would increase its contribution to both historical and
ecumenical understanding. The present volume is the result.

As conference secretary, I must fulfill the final duty of giving
special thanks to those whose efforts made the conference a success.
In addition to the speakers, chairmen, and commentators who are
listed on the program, let me say a word of thanks to Miss Nancy
Zuger of Fordham University who invented the idea; to Professor
Wilhelm Pauck, of Union Theological Seminary and Vanderbilt
University, who played a major role in shaping the program and
enticing participants. Acknowledgments are also due to the members
of the program committee: Professors Robert Handy and James D.
Smart of Union, Rev. Albert J. Loomie, s.j., Rev. Robert E. McNally,
s.j., Dr. John C. Olin, and Miss Nancy Zuger of Fordham. Mrs.
Ann Paul, Mr. James Prior, Mrs. Robert Craig and Miss Mae Gautier
rendered valuable service in arranging the thousand details which
made the conference a success. Finally, credit is due to Presidents
John C. Bennett and Leo P. McLaughlin, s.j., for the warm support
of this and other cooperative ventures, and to Dr. Merrimon
Cuninggim of the Danforth Foundation for encouraging both the
conference and this publication with the necessary material support.

ROGER WINES
Chairman, Department of History,
Fordham University
Conference Secretary

REFORMATION CONFERENCE PROGRAM

Friday, October 20, 1967   Fordham University
3:00 P.M. (Scholars and Students)
> Greetings: Roger Wines, Chairman, Fordham University History Department

ERASMUS AND THE REFORMATION

Introduction: Albert J. Loomie, s.j., Chairman; "Some Last Words of Erasmus" by Margaret Mann Phillips; "Erasmus and St. Ignatius Loyola" by John C. Olin; Commentators: James McConica, John Booty

---

8:00 P.M. (General Public Invited)
REAPPRAISAL OF THE REFORMATION
Introduction: James J. Hennesey, s.j., Chairman; "A Catholic View" by Robert E. McNally, s.j.; "The Problem of Authority in the Reformation" by Roland H. Bainton; Commentators: Paul Lehmann, John C. Olin

---

Saturday, October 21, 1967   Union Theological Seminary
10:00 A.M. (Scholars and Students)
> Greetings: John C. Bennett, President, Union Theological Seminary

LUTHER AS CONSERVER AND INNOVATOR

Introduction: James D. Smart, Chairman; "The Catholic Luther" by Wilhelm Pauck; "The Essential Luther" by John T. McDonough; Commentators: Edward D. McShane, s.j., John T. McNeill

2:00 P.M. (Scholars and Students)

LAY RECEPTION OF THE REFORMATION

Introduction: Cyril C. Richardson, Chairman; "The Princes and Protestantism" by Hajo Holborn; "Protestantism in the Cities" by Harold J. Grimm; Commentators: George Williams, Robert Kingdon

PROGRAM COMMITTEE: James D. Smart, Union Theological Seminary
Roger Wines, History Department, Fordham University

INTRODUCTION

ROBERT E. McNALLY, s.j.

On October 31, 1967, Western Christianity observed the 450th anniversary of the posting of the ninety-five theses by Martin Luther. Regardless of the diverse interpretations which Church historians and theologians have given to this event, the protest which those theses heralded was of sufficient symbolical value to merit in our day a solemn commemoration. For from this ordinary appeal to ecclesiastical authority against the abuse of religion by the sale of indulgences, there developed an unprecedented series of happenings which terminated ultimately in the disruption of Christendom and in the division of Christianity. What started in low key in Wittenberg, an obscure corner of the Holy Roman Empire, soon filled the Western World with its volume, and its echo continues to vibrate even centuries later. The events of the past cannot be erased nor should they; from them the present is born and takes its shape.

To grasp historical development as an organic process is an indispensable condition for understanding the anatomy of the Christian problematic that the Reformation poses to our day. In *The Future of Man*, Pierre Teilhard de Chardin has defined the role of history in human knowledge this way:

> It is clear in the first place that the world in its present state is the outcome of movement. Whether we consider the rocky layers enveloping the earth, the arrangement of the forms of life that inhabit it, the variety of civilizations to which it has given birth, or the structure of languages spoken upon it, we are forced to the same conclusion: that everything is the sum of the past and that nothing is comprehensible except through its history.[1]

Historical scholarship, therefore, is especially relevant in understand-

I

ing both the Reformation as an historical event and contemporary Christianity as "the sum of the past."

The pages of history which record the moving events of the Reformation are not completed, nor is the book which contains them sealed conclusively. As an historical happening, the Reformation has not yet found a definitive terminus. Its place, therefore, within the context of salvation history, where God draws His people into a unity and leads them upward and onward, is not clearly fixed. The special Providence which presides over human history ultimately reveals the finality of its purpose in the shape of history itself. In the end the faithful will write in word and deed the last chapter of the story, and in the light of this final chapter, when written, the definitive meaning of the past four centuries of Church history will appear. For the moment we are left to puzzle over the mystery of God's power, at once constructive and destructive, in the development of His Church on earth.

An anniversary is the commemorative observance of an historical event or person truly deserving recall by posterity. What happened *then* and *there* in the context of the past is remembered *here* and *now* in the circumstances of the present. Only those events and persons whose influence continues to radiate are celebrated. They have determined the lines of development on which the contemporary world moves. They have provided new points of departure, new insights and new possibilities still relevant and worthy of consideration after centuries. In the frame of history Martin Luther meets these qualifications. The medieval world in which he was born in 1483 was well nigh finished when he died in 1546. And though this transition from the old to the new order of things was not totally his doing, it was largely inspired by ideas and values which were born and nurtured in the spiritual milieu of his new concept of Christianity. Luther, therefore, is a maker of history; he shares in historical greatness as the father of the Reformation, an event to which each Christian, whatever his particular persuasion, is in some way related. He may accept or repudiate its central message; but he cannot be indifferent to it.

In retrospect "the affair" of the young Martin Luther (1517–21) might seem to be regrettable. What started on an academic level and in a provincial way should have terminated on that level and in that way. It did not, however. Rather it spiraled in importance. Under the impetus of canon law in the hands of those who overestimated the effectiveness of its power while underestimating the explosive force of the indulgence protest, a crisis developed which ultimately took on significance in world history. In his initial letter of October 31, 1517, to Archbishop Albrecht of Hohenzollern, Luther specified certain outstanding abuses which were connected with the preaching of indulgences and which of their nature required special attention. "There is sold," he wrote, " in the country under the protection of your illustrious name the papal indulgences for the building of St. Peter's in Rome."[2] The preaching of indulgences did not rest on sound theology; Albrecht's Instructions to the preachers were of questionable orthodoxy, at least in some important respects; superstition was being fostered among the simple people; the Gospel was neglected. In this context Luther posed an ominous question to the archbishop:

> What can I do, Most Sublime Bishop and Illustrious Elector, but to beseech you, through our Lord Jesus Christ, to cast your eyes of paternal care on this matter, to do away with these Instructions, and to order the indulgence preachers to preach differently? Otherwise someone may arise to contradict publicly the preachers and the Instructions, thereby bringing you into obliquity. This I deeply dread and yet I fear that something will happen soon unless the matter is taken care of.[3]

As history shows, the matter which deeply concerned Luther was not "taken care of" by the authority to which he appealed, and his deep dread that "something will happen" was justified in the sequel.

The abuses which clustered around the preaching of indulgences could have been swept away at once. But measures, adequate to the task, would have had to be drastic, if they were to achieve their effect. They would have required a vigorous reformer, a man at once shrewd and heroic. Albrecht was neither. He preferred to follow the law and its prescriptions as a secure and certain approach to the problem which confronted him. The legal process which he instituted against Luther became in due time a cause célèbre, agitated by tensions which grew beyond human control. In the passion of controversy both Luther and his opponents were forced into positions, at times extreme and unbalanced, from which departure with honor became impossible. Language grew immoderate; defiance was added to defiance. Compromise was out of the question. It was not part of the spirit of that age to be tolerant where Christian faith and morals were in question. If Luther seemed to know all the answers, so, too, did his adversaries. Thus the religious atmosphere became heavy with suspicion, resentment and mistrust. There came to be no room for a benign entente between Rome and Wittenberg.

Theological positions—Roman Catholic and Evangelical Protestant—solidified at an early date, even years before the Council of Trent (1545–63) had assembled. The primordial problematic of the debate—the theology of indulgences and their abuse—was soon forgotten as the confessional polemic developed; new questions, new issues and new problems came to the fore, often born from concrete historical situations. Almost from the beginning of his public career it became apparent that Martin Luther had defined the central issue of the Catholic-Lutheran debate for centuries to come. Then as now the problematic centered on the true understanding of the Church of Christ, its origins, its function, its character, and its relation to Gospel and ministry. Catholics would neither reject nor modify their traditional ecclesiology which the Protestants on the basis of their understanding of Holy Scripture refused to accept.

By the mid-sixteenth century it was evident that Western Christianity was fragmented into a plurality of communities. The post-Tridentine age witnessed no amelioration of the intransigence that marked the sharp division between Catholic and Evangelical Christians. The development of the terms "Roman Catholic"— which excessively accentuated the papal element—and "Lutheran" —which found no favor with Luther himself—only tended to widen the gap that was developing between the two churches. A most marked characteristic of this period, which unfortunately has been labeled Counter-Reformation, was a large-scale religious offensive on the Catholic side. This only underlined what was long apparent.

The Protestants were alienated from and irreconcilable to the Roman community. After the Treaty of Westphalia (1648) a pall of silence fell over these separated and hostile groups. Where there was dialogue, it was harshly polemical and narrowly confessional, carried on in a climate congenial to accusation and counter-accusation.

And, of course, prayer in common between these two believing and worshipping communities was out of the question. For the Lutheran the Mass, the central act of Roman Catholic worship, was an abomination, a distortion of Scripture, an act of idolatry. He coud have no part in it. Nor could the Catholic have any part in Lutheran worship, for *communicatio in sacris* was considered an act of superstition—the worship of the true God in a false way. Nothing brings out more clearly the hysteria of the past than the dread of contagion and infection which seized on both communities where there was question of common worship. Even a simple recital of the Lord's Prayer or the reading of Holy Scripture in common created conscience problems. How deeply alienated from one another Christians became in the Reformation period is well illustrated by the words of the English woman Bl. Margaret Clitherow (d. 1586) to the Anglican divines who offered to pray with her before her cruel death: "I will not pray with you, nor shall you pray with me; neither will I say Amen to your prayers, nor shall you to mine."[4]

This was the substantial heritage which the first half of this century inherited from the past. It was indeed the culmination of a tradition that was tendentious, divisive and separatist. The story of these difficult centuries is well known to every student of Church history. To affix moral responsibility and to measure the degrees of guilt of our forefathers is neither possible nor desirable. Moral censure for the lack of love and understanding falls more on the organized communities than on their individual members who were caught up by unreasonable passion and feeling that were part and parcel of the time and that were more often partisan than Christian. This is a classical example of man conditioned and victimized by the *Zeitgeist*.

But of prime importance in evaluating the spirit of the post-Tridentine development of Christianity is the growing loss of awareness that both Catholic and Protestant stem from a common mother—the medieval Church. In the heat of confessional debate theological differences were stressed and overstressed. Similarities were neglected and ignored. The lack of proper focus produced unbalanced, distorted images, at times caricature. Forgotten, or underestimated, in the polemical exchange was the realization that both communities shared in the precious Christian heritage—saving faith in Jesus Christ and His Gospel. The most consequential result of the Protestant–Catholic debate of these past centuries was alienation of Christian from Christian within the whole believing family of Christ which is the Church. The conviction grew that the two communities, though affirming the Gospel, were essentially different species of believers who had nothing in common, and precious little, if anything, to share with one another.

In reappraising the Reformation, especially in evaluating the current state of the question, two elements are of considerable importance. First, a rapprochement between Catholic and Protestant has been reached under the inspiration of the ecumenical movement. This was inconceivable a generation ago at the last great Lutheran anniversary, October 31, 1917. Second, the conviction that this rapprochement can be expressed in dialogue, in an open, sincere exchange of ideas both historical and theological, advances the cause of Christian unity on all levels and heralds a new chapter in Reformation history. Motivated by these considerations, a group of Protestant and Catholic scholars presented a symposium on the anniversary of the Lutheran theses; it was held under the auspices of Fordham University and the Union Theological Seminary of New York, with the support of the Danforth Foundation. The papers which are contained in this volume were delivered at this important anniversary celebration.

It is not necessary in this brief introduction to refer specifically to the individual essays nor to evaluate the contributions which each makes. The several papers speak for themselves. Obviously the range of themes which they cover is not comprehensive; but their scope is sufficiently broad to provide a rich variety of insights into the Reformation. If the center of interest is largely historical and theological, that derives from the nature of the anniversary which is celebrated. This book is presented as a contribution both to Church history and to historical theology. In a sense, then, it may be said to pose more questions than it answers. If it does, it will perform the valuable service of stimulating research in this area of scholarship and of creating new incentive to ecumenical dialogue. At any rate, the themes which make up the contents of this book are sufficiently important to merit here consideration and reflection.

The Reformation was an historical event, but it was even more than that. The inner values around which it centred its interest were deeply religious in character and transcended the movement of history. Its preoccupation was the reform not so much of moral corruption as of doctrinal decay. At issue was the meaning of the Gospel, its message of redemption and the means of salvation. To the reformers of the sixteenth century the medieval Church under the weight of history had become encumbered with archaic survivals, with contingent accretions that obliterated her true character and distracted from her true mission. In consequence, the Gospel was lost in an intricate maze of non-essentials; its efficacy was impaired. In their eyes the Church had failed as an authentic herald of the Word of God; either she did not preach it, or, if she did, she misunderstood the essential significance of its teaching. In view of these considerations, especially in view of Christianity as a religion ever to be renewed, the Reformation was historically necessary. It demanded that the hidden Gospel be once again restored to men, and that this restoration be bought at whatever cost to the Church and her traditions. Thus the reformers proposed to scale the Middle Ages with the hope of rediscovering the continuity of the Church with the Gospel in primitive Christianity.

Catholics, on the other hand, while freely conceding the urgency of restoring the long-neglected Gospel, were appalled at the violence which the Reformation had inflicted on Christian tradition and at the tragic schism that rent the unity of Christianity. The need for reform was generally admitted, even demanded, by those Churchmen who were intimately acquainted with the contemporary scene, especially in Germany; but the method, the path which true reform should follow in the prosecution of its goal, was hotly debated. The most liberal-minded Catholics of the time stood for a progressive renewal which would indeed revitalize the Church, without, however, detaching her from the past. Historical continuity was of prime importance to the Catholic reformer. In his thinking Christian tradition was an unbroken *continuum* linking past and present; it was living and unified, and it resided in the mind of the Church. To destroy this chain would be to cut the Church off from her source of life. Hence the Catholics came to dread the consequences of the Reformation.

Both Catholic and Protestant appealed to the Gospel as fundamental to their Christian confession; the former approached the sacred text through the Church and her tradition; the latter approached the Church and its tradition in the light of Holy Scripture, bringing them under its judgment. "The Book" was paramount; its authority unquestioned, because it was God's Word. But the interpretation of its message was the crucial issue. It posed a prime epistemological problem. For the method by which the believer discovers God's living revelation is basic to the character of what might be called the Catholic and the Protestant mind; it is a decisive principle of separation between the two. The Catholic hermeneutic suffered the risk of developing into a sheer voluntarism that would substitute the authority of the Church for the authority of the Word. The Protestant position had its own dangers. Its emphasis on the authority of the Scriptures could lead to a blindness concerning the Church's necessary function as interpreter, and so in fact it did open the way to a disruptive individualism. With growing irritation Luther witnessed this development; for this was a development which, unless properly disciplined, could inevitably displace Holy Scripture from its place of privilege. That Catholics and Protestants read the same Gospel texts under the guidance of the same Spirit and derived opposite meanings is a paradox. And this paradox underscores the difficulties inherent in any appeal to Church or Spirit, where the sense of Scripture is at issue.

Luther was a Protestant, at least in the eyes of his Catholic opponents. He repudiated the Holy See, for example, and he also repudiated conciliar authority. He was solemnly excommunicated and was no longer in communion with the Roman Catholic world. He was indeed a Protestant, but he was not simply a Protestant. Born in the late medieval world, he matured in its traditions and was thoroughly impregnated by its atmosphere. More than half his life was lived in the Catholic community, and he was nurtured by its sacraments, its authority, spirituality, books and art. Even had he wished, he could not have divested himself of these Catholic influences which continued to be part of his *Weltanschauung* until the day he died. Luther's total spiritual and intellectual formation is a classical example illustrating the continuity of history.

The Reformation involved a schism, but not in the sense that Luther envisioned the foundation of a new Church in opposition to the old one. The sharp dialectic that led on to the schism is far too complicated to be discussed here, nor need it be. No Reformation scholar can overlook the fact that in a very real sense Luther remained Catholic while breaking with Rome. Obviously he did not remain nor did he wish to remain a formal member of the community which had harshly repudiated and excluded him on January 3, 1521. But in many of his theological thought patterns, in the spiritual values which he treasured, and in the religious attitudes which characterize him, the Catholic tradition and influence are manifest. The sum of his life and of his life's work contains side by side the new and the old, the one interpreting, completing, and shedding light on the other. This facet of Luther as reformer must not be overlooked in evaluating Reformation history. The fullness of its significance is not yet fully appreciated.

In a sense, therefore, Luther was Catholic. The Church to which he belonged, from which his career sprang, and which he wished to reform, was Roman Catholic. But what was the essential Luther? Was he Protestant or Catholic? In the light of history the question seems scarcely valid; if it be valid, its answer is difficult, for he was not so much at extremes either the one or the other. Above all else Martin Luther was a Christian, a reformer, and a zealot who was caught up in an intricate web of circumstances that the vigor of his thought could not control. Invariably his work was under strain and compulsion, and in an atmosphere of crisis. He was a man of the Gospel; on it he built his concept of Christianity. But he was an isolated man who labored in the narrow context of his own inspirations and insights, perhaps too much apart from Christian tradition, too much fixed on the sacred text as a personal discovery. In the span of a short lifetime he attempted to accomplish the work of centuries. His pedagogy could not support the weight of his message. Through his voice and pen came division. If "Luther is partly responsible for saving the Church" (McDonough), he saved it by dividing it. This is the essential paradox of his Reformation.

The questions posed by Martin Luther fomented a theological debate which the printing press carried to all parts of Europe. It engaged the attention of the Catholic hierarchy from pope in Rome to parish priest in the backwoods, and it soon became a matter of deep concern to the university faculties of theology which were expected to pronounce *ex officio* on the issues at stake. But the essential Reformation was neither solely theological nor solely academic; to a large degree it was a religious movement which rested on the laity—on the princes, therefore, and on the urban classes, the patricians and the artisans of the free imperial cities of Germany. If the Reformation was a revolution (and it was to a certain degree), its success ultimately depended on its ability to capture the heart and mind of the *agora*; for without the consensus of the majority of men no reform movement can achieve its essential purpose. Failure is more subtle. What if the majority supports the exterior form of a reform movement—its ways and means—while neglecting its inner spirit which must be charity?

The pure ideals of a reformer are never realized in the spirit in which they were first conceived. In the case of Martin Luther it was not simply a matter of unlocking the Gospel and allowing it to run its victorious course. He spoke that way, but he knew better. No different from the reform of the Tridentine popes, his work was simultaneously helped and hindered by the territorial princes of the Empire whose range of vision, personal motivation, and degree of commitment were often questionable. What the role of princes should be in the Church and its reformation was clear to Luther, at least in theory; it was not always clear to them in practice. In the relation of Christian princes to ecclesiastical community, as the reformers structured it, there is an irritating ambiguity that requires further clarification, particularly since "the fate of German Protestantism was decided by the princes" (Holborn).

It is simply a matter of fact that in every German city there were important men, politicians and humanists, who embraced the Reformation almost from the outset. In this they were joined and supported by urban artisans and guildsmen, not universally but to a degree that was to prove decisive. Ultimately a significant percentage of these free imperial cities and their citizens adhered to the Reformation, "a folk movement, touching all segments of society" (Grimm). The townsmen were modern and progressive; they were more than touched by the new humanism, and they entertained a serious interest in religion and religious questions. In a sense they were ripe for the Reformation, and were ready and eager to profit economically and socially from the implications of its theology. The important part that the townsmen played in the Reformation illustrates the fact that it was not a predominantly clerical affair, a movement solely sustained and carried by churchmen and theologians. Tired of the Church, as they knew it, the towns looked elsewhere for new inspiration. They found it in the Reformation.

Humanists joined the ranks of the reformers. Erasmus, the humanist par excellence, did not. While recognizing in Luther "a fierce sincerity and a true devotion to religion" (Phillips), he did not share his essential convictions nor would he affiliate himself with his Reformation. Erasmus was independent; and this independence put him in the middle of two contending forces. He was not accepted by the Protestants (nor did he wish to be), yet the harshly critical style and manner in which he addressed himself to Church problems alienated many Catholics from him. He was a shrewd man, a keen observer and critic of the foibles of Christian life. But no consideration of the low state of the Church, the decadent morality which he saw on all sides, the exhausted theology which surrounded the faith, could persuade him to go over to the Reformation. On this he was adamant. Essentially he stood for a purified Church living according to the spirit of the Gospel, a Church of simplicity and charity informed by the true wisdom of Jesus Christ.

As Catholic and humanist, Erasmus was at once man of the Church and proponent of reform. On behalf of both he worked tirelessly according to his own unique method. His subsequent influence on the intellectual and spiritual life of Europe was considerable, directly or indirectly touching a whole generation of churchmen, scholars, and men of affairs. To situate Ignatius Loyola in the orbit of Erasmus might seem at first to be going beyond what the facts of the matter allow. He was "not an Erasmian in the usual sense of that term" (Olin). Still no definitive wall separated the two nor were their spirits simply opposed. Erasmianism was in the air, and Ignatius could not have helped breathing it in, transforming it in accord with his own specific purpose. The simplicity of the ascetical life which he described for his followers, his insistence on the acquisition of solid virtue and humanistic learning as fundamental, and his radical departure from the monastic and mendicant tradition gave new dignity to religious life at a time when its existence was imperiled. "With one decisive gesture" he accepted "the heart of Christian humanism—the renewal of theology through a return to Holy Scripture and the Fathers" (Olin). Studied from this point of view, Ignatius emerges as a positive reformer whose thinking was deeply influenced by the humanistic movement inspired by Erasmus.

The eight essays which make up this volume are presented here in the spirit in which they were originally conceived. As a contribution to Reformation studies, they represent different attitudes, different insights, and different conclusions. In enriching their understanding of the Reformation of the sixteenth century, scholars must engage in open dialogue, in a frank exchange and counter-exchange of ideas. This is especially true of an epoch as complicated and delicate as the period under discussion in this book. Before we can understand the significance of what is happening now, we must appreciate the significance of what happened then. In the mirror of the past the present is reflected. This process of clarification is fundamental; it will inevitably lead to a new interpretation of the Reformation, and thereby to a new appreciation of our Christian heritage, the ultimate basis on which both Catholic and Protestant must stand.

NOTES

1. P. Teilhard de Chardin, *The Future of Man* (New York, 1964), p. 12.
2. H. J. Hillerbrand, *The Reformation* (New York, 1964), p. 50.
3. *Ibid.*, pp. 50–51.
4. M. T. Munro, *Blessed Margaret Clitherow* (New York, 1947), p. 101. Mary Claridge, *Margaret Clitherow* (New York, 1966), p. 174.

The Problem of Authority in the Age of the Reformation

ROLAND H. BAINTON

THE THORNIEST PROBLEM of the Reformation is that of authority. It is also a divisive force today. If my memory serves me rightly, when one of the Protestant observers at the Second Vatican Council was exuberantly enthusiastic with regard to immediate reunion, Cardinal Bea himself issued a caution, saying, "Remember, there is the question of authority." This authority is of two kinds. There is jurisdictional authority, under which some person or group must make decisions and ask compliance if there is to be corporate action. The other variety rests on a claim to truth. Those who believe that they have the truth demand obedience. Those who are not persuaded that the makers of the claim are right refuse obedience. The papacy in the sixteenth century asserted both kinds of authority. Some believers were ready to concede to the papacy the authority of jurisdiction, provided it were dissociated from the claim to infallibility. Of such was Erasmus, and at the outset Luther also was deferential to the pope until he claimed too much.

The pretension to authority based on truth precipitated the most intense conflict. It raised at once the prior question of how truth can be ascertained. This had long been a tormenting problem for Christians because they operated with two views of the way to truth, the one derived from the Hellenic, the other from the Hebraic tradition. According to the one, truth is the goal of a quest; according to the other, the elucidation of a revelation. The one sees truth emerging from below, the other descending from above. The Greeks developed the former approach as to both science and philosophy. The scientific method calls for observation, classification, and interpretation by human intelligence. But since human intelligence is fallible the insights and findings of one observer must be subject to the criticisn and collaboration of others. Through this collaborative effort truth emerges. In the realm of philosophy the case is not entirely comparable because here one cannot collect, collate and interpret data in the same fashion. Truth may be said in a sense to come down from above in the form of innate ideas or special insights. But again the insights of one individual need to be checked by those of others. Insights must be shared and mutually examined. The manner of sharing is the dialogue. This is not simply a device for propagating ideas through disclosing the steps whereby an opponent is vanquished. No doubt, of course, Plato, when he actually composed his dialogues, knew how they would conclude; but one has the feeling that they are the records of discussions in which at the outset the end was open and each of the participants worked on the assumption that the other participants might be right

Agreement reached by such a process was credited with a claim to truth. The consensus of honest inquirers is an indication that they are right. This assumption is basic for the idea of natural law, a universal morality conceived in terms of what all peoples actually do. Such was the view of Aristotle. It is basic also for a natural theology consisting of what all peoples actually believe. Thus Cicero argued for the truth of God and immortality because in his day they were universally believed. The Stoics supplied a rational ground for the assumption by positing a universal principle of rationality in all men, the immanent logos. The consent of all men, the *consensus omnium*, has, therefore, a high degree of probability, though tinged with tentativeness and open to revision by a subsequent consensus.[1]

The view that truth comes down from above is Hebraic. In the realm of religion this truth is revelation. Moses received the commandments directly from the ·hand of God. The prophets thundered, "Thus saith the Lord." In the New Testament truth was sometimes conveyed through dreams, through the ecstatic experience of being caught up into the third heaven, by personal encounters with Him who was the way, the truth and the life, and by some profound inner conviction, so that Paul could say, "When God was pleased to reveal his Son to me."[2] A very significant difference between this Hebraic and the Hellenic view of the source of truth is that the revelation is not given to all men equally. The Master prayed, "I thank thee, Father, Lord of heaven and earth, that thou hast hid these things from the wise and understanding and revealed them to babes."[3] The Apostle Paul held that although from the creation of the world God had revealed Himself to the gentiles through the things which have been made, yet "their senseless minds were darkened and, claiming to be wise, they became fools."[4] God vouchsafed his special revelation to that tiny people, Israel, and when Israel was guilty of backsliding, then to a remnant within Israel. Christ showed Himself to the little flock who went in by the narrow gate, and, as Dean Inge well remarked, this gate was never inconveniently crowded. Cicero might argue for the existence of God and the reality of life after death by reason of universal belief. But one could not use this argument as proof of the resurrection, for this was a stumbling block to the Jew and folly to the gentile.[5] Following this line of thought one might conclude that the majority is always wrong.

Nevertheless in Christian thought the principle of consensus has been combined with the concept of revelation, not the consent of all men, but of illumined men, the babes to whom the wisdom has been given which is denied to the wise and understanding. The combination of the two approaches came about after Christian revelation had received a certain codification by reduction to writing in those books which were to form the New Testament. How should these books be interpreted? Differences of opinion arose especially between the orthodox and the Gnostics. Both appealed to tradition as the key to interpretation. The Gnostics affirmed that they were the custodians of a tradition going back through their leaders to Christ and the apostles. The orthodox asked to whom any such tradition was likely to have been committed if not to those whom the apostles appointed to succeed them in the governance of the churches and again to their successors. Thus the babes to whom the wisdom was given became the bishops. But suppose the bishops disagreed? Then the consensus of those who did agree was the norm—if not quite the *consensus omnium*, at any rate the *consensus* of nearly *omnium*. He was deemed to be within the Church who agreed with the bishops who agreed with each other. Such was the view of Cyprian. Even this view was severely shaken when Athanasius was *contra mundum*, against the world of the other bishops, but later deemed to have been right. Then the formula had to be stated with greater precision as the consensus of all, continuously and everywhere, *ab omnibus, semper et ubique*.

The question whether truth lies with the consensus of the majority or the insights of the minority within the Church became again acute in the age of the Reformation. A wide spectrum of opinion emerged both among those who remained with the Church of Rome and those who were cast out or withdrew. The extreme on the Catholic side was represented by Mazzolini, commonly known as Sylvester Prierias, Master of the Sacred Palace, commissioned by Pope Leo to reply to Martin Luther. Prierias said that "whoever does not accept the doctrine of the Roman Church and of the Roman pontiff as the infallible rule of faith from which sacred Scripture derives strength and authority is a heretic." Luther retorted by denying the infallibility of popes and of councils and asserting the sole authority of Scripture. In his *Address to the Christian Nobility* Luther attacked the doctrine of papal infallibility as the utter reversal of the principle of consensus. To make of one man the sole interpreter of Scripture is the very pinnacle of individualism. And by what token is he endowed with such power? If God spoke to the prophet Balaam through the mouth of an ass, why not through the mouth of any ordinary Christian? Yet Luther was not setting up the principle of the consensus of *all* ordinary Christians. He recognized the need for philological training in order to understand the meaning of the words of Scripture. Yet this of itself would not yield the true sense, for such learning is at the command of the new Scribes and Pharisees, the late scholastics, who by their sophisticated quiddities pervert the Word of God. If Luther were reminded that they constituted the majority, he countered by saying "The minority is always right," namely that minority which is able to discern the things of God because touched by the finger of God.[6] Such babes in Christ, even if dependent on translations of the Scriptures, may better grasp the import of God's Word than the wise and understanding with all their Greek and Hebrew, though these are not to be discarded.

In order to understand the Scriptures one must have the spirit. But what is it to have the spirit? Certainly the spirit connotes warmth, piety and empathy. But the spirit is not one's own individual spirit. It is the Holy Spirit, which spoke through the mouths of the prophets and evangelists. Therefore Scripture is to be interpreted by the spirit of Scripture. The interpreter must be in that spirit. Now the spirit of Scripture is not to be equated with the letter of Scripture. Within Scripture itself there are levels, according to Luther. The norm is the Word of God and the Word of God is the deed of God in redeeming the world through the incarnation and passion of His Son. That in Scripture which makes this proclamation is the Word within Scripture, because Scripture as such is not the Word of God. Scripture is like the manger in which the baby Jesus lay. The Baby is the Word. The manger holds the Word, and there is some straw in the manger too. Luther had a hierarchy of values within the Bible. In the New Testament he gave the first places to the Gospel of John and the main Pauline epistles. The synoptic gospels and the pastoral epistles were less esteemed. James and Revelation were viewed askance. In the Old Testament Luther preferred Genesis, where Abraham was saved by faith, and the Psalms which express the penitence of David. But Esther was to him a hateful book.

If then the norm within Scripture is the redeeming work of God, Scripture is clear. One passage interprets another. This was precisely the point at which opponents assailed Luther, in particular Erasmus who contended that many passages in Scripture are very far from clear, as, for example, the nature of the unforgivable sin. All the apparatus of technical scholarship does not suffice to clarify some points, nor does Luther's principle clear up a passage like this. How then is the meaning to be discerned? Erasmus said that he would defer to the authority of the Church because it rested upon the *consensus omnium*, that is the continuing consensus of the Fathers and the councils. Some Catholics advanced the further argument that the Church should interpret Scripture because the Church made Scripture. In the beginning of Christianity there was no specifically Christian Scripture. Members of the Church wrote the books which were to become the New Testament. The judgment of the Church selected the books. Thus the Church made the gospel. The reformers replied that the Word of God, the redeeming work of God in Christ, made the Church. The Church, then, recorded the Word of God in Scripture, and the Church itself is to be judged by that recorded Word which any Christian can understand.

For the Catholics the problem was, who speaks for the Church? Some answered, the pope. Erasmus did not. Thomas More did not. The appeal was rather to the consensus of the Christian interpreters, particularly the Fathers of the Church. Erasmus would give a high place to Church councils if confirmed by subsequent tradition. He said that he could easily have been a Pelagian or an Arian if the Church had not ruled otherwise. The Church had ruled otherwise, and he bowed to her judgment. Luther refused to bow. When Cajetan confronted him with the papal bull on the theory of indulgences, a bull incorporated into canon law, Luther flatly rejected it. He was not insensitive, however, to the force of tradition. The examiner at Worms asked him how he dared to call into question the most holy orthodox faith instituted by Christ, proclaimed by the apostles, sealed by the blood of the martyrs, confirmed by the sacred councils, defined by the Church, and given by the pope and the emperor to be believed, not discussed. Luther responded with his famous, unequivocal answer. But when subsequently alone in the asylum of the Wartburg the question plagued him: "Are you alone wise? Have so many centuries gone wrong?" Reassurance came through a renewed study of the Scriptures. Their meaning was plain, no matter how many failed to see it.

Then Erasmus came at him again. How to be certain with respect to the meaning of Scripture was the most crucial question in their debate on the freedom of the will. As a matter of fact they were not so far apart on that issue as they supposed. Erasmus assumed that Luther regarded man as an automaton, which he did not, for he recognized that even the Turk and the Jew are free to be good parents and good magistrates. But man's nature is such that he can never be perfect. At some point he will fail. For his salvation he must, therefore, depend solely on the grace of God. Erasmus quite agreed. But he objected to the doctrine of predestination. Logically he ought not to have done so because it is implied in the doctrine of justification by faith to which he gave assent. For if they alone are saved who have faith and if faith is a gift of God not granted to all, then predestination necessarily follows. Erasmus did not perceive the logic and affirmed simply that if God saved some and damned others without regard to merit or demerit then God is a tyrant.

Luther replied that he had more than once been cast down to the very abyss of desperation by this reflection, but he was compelled to accept it because it is grounded in Scripture. But where in Scripture? asked Erasmus. Luther directed him to the ninth chapter of Paul's letter to the Romans, where the apostle, quoting Genesis, says that God "hardened Pharaoh's heart." Erasmus replied that this does not mean that God made Pharaoh's heart hard but that he gave him repeated opportunities of showing how hard it was. Luther pointed to another passage in which before even the twins were born God said, "Jacob I loved, but Esau I hated." Erasmus interpreted this statement as due to God's foreknowledge rather than to His predestination. In justification of his exegesis Erasmus appealed to the consensus of the early Fathers. In the case of the verse about Pharaoh the explanation was taken from Origen, but not in the other instance because Origen accounted for the judgments on Jacob and Esau on the ground of their prenatal behavior. All of the other early Fathers employed the device of foreknowledge except Augustine. Erasmus could say to Luther than the consensus is to be followed.

Yet, as a matter of fact, Erasmus himself adhered to this principle only with respect to questions which he deemed insoluble or inconsequential. When it came to matters about which he was deeply convinced, and they were all ethical, he did not hesitate to diverge. This was true as to his pacifism. He could appeal to a consensus only down to the time of Constantine. Notably Origen, the favorite of Erasmus, was a pacifist and no Church Father before Constantine condoned Christian participation in actual warfare. But after Constantine Eusebius did not condemn the military exploits which had ended the persecution. Ambrose began soon to clamor for a crusade against the heretical Goths, and Augustine formulated the doctrine of the just war which had enjoyed the support of the consensus for more than a thousand years up to the time of Erasmus. On the subject of divorce Erasmus broke entirely with the tradition of canon law. The Church held to the word of Christ in Matthew's gospel that there should be no divorce save for adultery. Erasmus spiritualized adultery, for, said he, adultery of the spirit is worse than that of the flesh. That being so, he would allow divorce for what we might call incompatibility. He certainly did not allow himself to be hampered by the consensus.

Luther in the meantime was aghast to discover that his principle did not lead to unanimity of interpretation even among his own followers. Others who also claimed to be interpreting Scripture in accord with the spirit of Scripture did not agree with him as to particular points. There were Carlstadt and Zwingli, who denied the real physical presence of Christ in the mass. Luther appealed to the words of institution, "This is my body." And if this is not sufficient, then there is that other word of Paul, "The cup of blessing which we bless, is it not the communion of the blood of Christ? The bread which we break, is it not the communion of the body of Christ?" "This," said Luther, "is the Donnerschlag, the thunderclap to demolish Carlstadt and Zwingli." Carlstadt and Zwingli spiritualized the sacrament. Luther took the words of Paul literally; the Sacramentarians, as they were called, spiritually.

But the case was reversed with respect to images. Here Carlstadt and Zwingli took literally the command to make no likeness of anything in the heavens above, the earth beneath, or the waters under the earth. Luther said that this command was intended only for the Jews because of their propensity for idolatry. In order to take the edge off the commandment Luther treated it as an appanage of the first injunction "Thou shalt have no other gods before me," and not as the second commandment, as in the Reformed churches. In order to keep the total number of the commandments at ten Luther had to make two out of the prohibitions of covetousness at the end of the list. The reason for the difference of interpretation on the part of Luther and Carlstadt and Zwingli may well be sought in a basic difference as to the relation of body and spirit. Luther was genuinely Catholic in his materialism, that is to say in his readiness to use the material as a vehicle for the spiritual. Carlstadt and Zwingli saw the physical as an impediment and wished to dispense with external aids to religion. For this reason Luther subscribed to the view that Christ is physically present on the altar and was willing to use sensory symbols. Carlstadt and Zwingli rejected both. Despite the claim to interpret Scripture only by the spirit of Scripture, presuppositions affected exegesis.

Then came those in Luther's camp who made so much of the spirit as to disparage the Scripture entirely. The Zwickau prophets claimed to have had conversations with God. Luther put no credence in their celestial chattings. "Divine Majesty does not speak directly to men. God is a consuming fire." Next appeared Thomas Müntzer, appealing to dreams, visions and portents, and emptying the vials of scorn on Luther's biblicism. "What good is it to have swallowed the Bible one hundred thousand times" if one has not known the new birth in the spirit? The Word of God is not on paper but in the heart. Away then with the mere book! "Bible, Babel, bubble," Müntzer cried. Luther replied that unless Müntzer could produce a plain word of Scripture he would not listen to him, though he had swallowed the Holy Ghost, feathers and all. Müntzer was declaring that truth is derived from direct, inner, personal religious experience. He claimed for himself as a prophet even more than the Church of Rome claimed for the pope. The source of truth is revelation directly given in the present. He who has this revelation is able to open the Scriptures because he is in the spirit in which the Scriptures were given. But he does not need the Scriptures. This is to dissociate Christianity from history. Luther stoutly protested. For him Christianity dates from a unique event, the self-disclosure of God in Jesus Christ. If the Spirit speaks today just as plainly, with as much authority, just as profoundly as in the days of Christ and the apostles, then Christianity ceases to be rooted in history. In that case it is no longer Christianity, for it cannot retain its character if turned into a merely contemporary cult by the visions of fanatics or the individualism of popes, who, just as much as the fanatics, pretend to a monopoly on the Holy Ghost.

Finally, there were those like Sebastian Franck who also inveighed against the letter; but not in favor of the spirit in terms of visions or portents, but rather in the form of mystical experience. For them the Bible is significant as a mythology of the spirit. Everything described in outward terms has only an inner meaning. The birth of Christ signifies His birth in me; the passion is the *via dolorosa* for me on the earthly pilgrimage; the resurrection is the renewal of the spirit in union with the Ultimate. Here again history is denuded of all temporal significance. For such an attitude Luther had no use. Obviously it has roots in medieval Catholic mysticism, by which Luther was not permanently influenced.

This brief analysis may serve to show that the problem of authority was not simply a matter of confessional difference. Catholics were divided. Protestants were divided. Subsequently the Catholics have become more united, particularly since the first Vatican Council which decreed papal infallibility. But since the second Vatican there are not a few Catholics who appear to find that doctrine an embarrassment. One of them said to me, "You Protestants take the doctrine of papal infallibility altogether too seriously. It doesn't mean a thing, because given the ambiguities of language there is no infallible way in which infallibility can be communicated."

As for the Protestants, they are earnestly questing for truth in religion, a truth compatible with everything else which man has come to know by way of empirical investigation. That being so, what should be the attitude of Christians of any confession to jurisdictional authority? Catholics, until recently at any rate, have believed that they should submit to authority, and if, for example, the Church refuses permission to publish their findings, scholars should put their manuscripts back into their desks and wait for time and God to give them vindication. The Protestant on the other hand is committed to the method of reaching truth by way of dialogue (liberal Protestants, at any rate). Consequently he who thinks he has an insight or has made a discovery should not deprive the world of his findings but should bring them forth to be refuted or confirmed. This principle prompted Lessing, for example, to publish the Reimarus fragments. Curiously this is an Erasmian principle. He gave an analysis of how truth is hammered out by the matching of minds. There are admittedly, said he, periods of retrogression in this process while winter harbors the seeds of spring. There appear to be negations because each generation of scholars reacts against the preceding, yet each may have a true insight not perceived by those who went before. The sum of the findings appears to be discordant, but nothing could be more concordant through the coincidence of opposites. Here Erasmus comes out with the formula of Nicolas of Cusa. The moral is that throughout this entire process investigation and expression should be untrammeled. This was not Luther's reason for speaking out. He was not engaging in a tentative quest. He was proclaiming the eternal truth of God. He would not be silent. Erasmus, despite his commitment to open discussion, told Luther that, having been condemned by the Church and the Empire, he should subside. Another consideration also entered here: Luther's continued agitation was disrupting the peace of the Church and of Christendom. Wars of religion were already beginning. Let Luther be silent in the interests of peace, and for the sake of that atmosphere in which alone discussion can prove fruitful. When tempers are so heated, silence is better than violence of word or deed. This was the consideration which induced Schwenckfeld to declare a moratorium on the celebration of the Eucharist until it could be observed without acrimony. Luther's reply to Erasmus was, "You with your peace-loving theology, you don't care about truth. Suppose the world does go to smash. God can make another world." Luther was insisting that the truth which comes down from above is not to be hidden. Erasmus was saying that the truth which is worked out from below does not distill at a high temperature.

————————

At the close of this lecture I was asked whether I believe that silence is better than violence of word or deed. I answered that circumstances must be considered. A man under attack may refrain from a reply rather than set off a chain reaction of recriminations. When men find themselves unable to carry on a discussion in a reasonable manner, with readiness on the part of each to listen to the other, they do well to declare a moratorium until they have achieved emotional control. If there is a monstrous abuse it must be exposed and denounced, but he who makes the exposure should refrain from wanton provocation and should seek to restrain his following from irresponsible violence of word and deed.

NOTES

Documentation of statements made in this paper can be found in my life of Luther entitled *Here I Stand* (New York, 1950), and more fully in an essay entitled "The Bible in the Reformation," *Cambridge History of the Bible* (Cambridge, 1963). Statements about Erasmus are documented in my biography of Erasmus recently published by Scribner's (New York, 1969) under the title *Erasmus of Christendom*. A few references in the foregoing paper call for notes:

1. Klaus Oehler, "Der *Consensus Omnium* als Kriterium der Wahrheit in der antiken Philosophie und der Patristik," *Antike und Abendland*, X (1961), 103–29.
2. Galatians 1:16.
3. Matthew 11:25.
4. Romans 1:21–22.
5. 1 Corinthians 1:23–24.
6. *D. Martini Luthers Werke* (Weimar, 1883–), VII, 317.

The Reformation: A Catholic Reappraisal

ROBERT E. McNALLY, s.j.

FOUR HUNDRED AND FIFTY years ago, on October 31, 1517, an obscure Augustinian friar signed, sealed, and dispatched a letter to the Primate of all Germany.[1] The friar, professor of Holy Scripture at the University of Wittenberg in Saxony, member—a conspicuously edifying member—of the Augustinian cloister in that town, learned scholar and religious priest was Martin Luther (1483–1546). The recipient of the letter was Albrecht of Hohenzollern (1490–1545), the Archbishop of Mainz and Prince Elector of the Holy Roman Empire, already one of the most influential and powerful churchmen in all Germany. Here in this letter was the beginning, small and obscure like a distant cloud, of an agonizing religious and political contest whose results were beyond all imagining. At the moment, no one (least of all Luther himself) sensed that the thrust of history had reached a new moment which would push on to an essential change in the structure of the Christian world as it was then known. The consequences of this letter remain with us to this day.

These two men, Martin Luther and Albrecht of Hohenzollern, were Catholic; they were obedient sons of the Church and loyal servants of the Holy See. They were relatively young men: the archbishop was twenty-seven; the friar, thirty-four. One was an ecclesiastical administrator, a man of affairs, accustomed to the chancery and ecclesiastical business; the other was a university professor, involved in pastoral ministry, already quite at home in the pulpit as well as in the lecture hall, and well on the way to a literary career.[2] The archbishop was scion of an illustrious family, the noble, rich and influential House of Hohenzollern. Luther, on the other hand, characterized his lineage this way: "I am the son of a peasant. My great-grandfather, grandfather and father were peasants."[3] Both men were Germanic to the core, born and raised in the autumn of the Middle Ages, and committed to the Church as a way of life. Neither was a saint, but neither was a devil. They were ordinary churchmen devoted to the work proper to their vocations. Neither was a trouble-maker; yet neither realized the vast historical troubles that would grow out of this epistolary confrontation.

Luther's letter to the archbishop was dispatched on October 31, 1517. It was marked received by his curia on November 17. We are fortunate in knowing both how and what Luther wrote to the primate of the German Church; and we are even more fortunate in being able to trace the development of "this little spark" into flames beyond the control of the whole civilized world. His letter was dignified, correct, polite, at times even obsequious[4]; but it was very much to the point, and the point was that the public sale of indulgences was in his eyes and in the eyes of his people an abuse of the Christian religion. He made one accurate observation:

> . . . Reverend Father in Christ, Most Illustrious Elector . . . there is sold in the country under the protection of your illustrious name the papal indulgence for the building of St. Peter's in Rome.[5]

He offered one shrewd piece of advice:

> It should be the foremost and only care of all bishops to teach the Gospel and love of Christ to the people. Christ nowhere commanded to preach indulgences, but emphatically insisted on the preaching of the Gospel.[6]

And, finally, he posed one embarrassing question:

> What great danger and shame wait for a bishop who allows the Gospel to be silenced, but suffers the pompous proclamation of indulgences and is more concerned about indulgences than the Gospel?[7]

The accurate observation was overlooked; the shrewd advice was neglected, and the embarrassing question was left unanswered.

Taken in its historical consequence, this letter may be one of the most significant Church letters since St. Paul wrote his last epistle. I say this, not because of the intrinsic value of what is written therein; the content of the text is quite ordinary, common and known for centuries. It is basically the kind of letter that indignant Christians often write to their bishops apropos of religious abuses which they have noted. Luther's letter, therefore, contains no profound theological insights nor does it propose religious innovations. It is, as he said himself, "a humble but faithful admonition." But from this letter, as an event, a happening and a symbol, a whole series of other events, happenings and symbols evolved that ultimately changed the character of Christendom. Fundamentally the letter was the desperate appeal of a peasant to a nobleman, of a friar to a bishop; but it was more than that. It was the appeal of a religious who happened to be a university professor, who had a mind of his own and knew how to express it, as the subsequent events proved.

The archbishop did not receive Luther's letter with indifference; it was not simply thrown into the dust-bin. There were legitimate ways and means to handle a case such as this, and the archbishop had every intention of using these ways and means.[8] Friar Luther in Wittenberg had written to Archbishop Albrecht in Mainz who in turn wrote to Pope Leo in Rome. This was a century of letter writers who accomplished vast quantities of business by the use of pen and ink; everyone had to have his say and everyone seemed to have the ink and pen to say it. They were men who greatly believed in the power of the word written, printed or spoken, and they poured it out in torrents.

Soon other letters from other quarters were written against Luther —to the Roman Curia and to Pope Leo X. Soon Luther was up to his neck in legal process and its red tape; he was trapped in a net of law in a century in which it was far more terrifying to fall into the hands of lawyers than into the hands of God. By the time the first dust wave had begun to settle (1521), Luther found himself excommunicated by the canon law and cast out by the civil law. Still he adhered to his theological position. He had protested the competence and validity of both pope and emperor, and thus became a "protestant"—a name which I do not think that he especially resented. But

I do feel that he would have resented the idea that his evangelical concept of Christianity should one day be called Lutheran.

It is one of the peculiarities of history that this simple friar, biblical professor and doctor of theology—a man whose life centered in the obscure University of Wittenberg—should have successfully resisted Pope Leo X (Giovanni de' Medici, of the most cultivated family in Europe), and Emperor Charles V, who characterized himself as descended from "the most Christian emperors of the illustrious German nation."[9] There is little wonder that Luther and his career have so intrigued the Western world that he has become one of the most-written-about personages in its history, and it is curious to note that in his own day he was represented by his admirers as another suffering Christ.[10] When in the days after the Diet of Worms Albrecht Dürer believed that Luther had died, he wrote: "O God, if Luther is dead, who will henceforth explain to us the Gospel? What might he not have written for us in the next ten or twenty years?"[11]

By some peculiar mystique ecclesiastical authority seems to act on the principle that Church problems solve themselves; or, if they really need a solution here and now, theological formulae, ascetical principles, or legal process will handle the matter. Luther had posed a problem to his archbishop; it was not really a difficult problem to solve, at least theoretically. Religion was being abused by a bad theology of indulgences and by the sale of indulgences; therefore, the sale of indulgences should have been halted and the bad theology at once corrected.[12] In fact, Luther had enclosed in the letter together with the theses "a short treatise sketching a tentative theology of indulgences."[13] This should have proved helpful. But authority ignored the problem, at least for the moment; when it finally decided to act, it elected canonical process as its method—canonical process not against the indulgence preachers who had created the scandal, but against the indulgence protestor who was creating an even greater scandal. History shows that this method failed miserably.

This is the way that Luther interpreted the affairs of October 31, 1517, when he wrote about the matter years later:

Your Electoral Grace will please remember the beginning (Oct. 31, 1517), and what a horrible fire was kindled by ignoring this little spark. The whole world was then surely of the opinion that one poor friar was too unimportant to receive the pope's attention and was undertaking an impossible task. But God decided to give the pope and all his followers more than enough to do. Over and against the opinion of the whole world, God directed the game to the point where the pope will hardly be able to straighten out this affair any more; in addition the pope's situation is daily growing worse, so that one may see the hand of God in this. . . .[14]

That is the way Luther saw the beginning of the "affair," or "the game," as he remarked cynically. Since October 31, 1517, God has indeed given "the pope and all his followers more than enough to do"; but perhaps Luther when he wrote: "the pope will hardly be able to straighten out this affair any more," concealed in these few words a certain unconscious optimism, however tenuous and obscure. The word "hardly" does not mean "never"; it means "possibly but with difficulty and hazard." It leaves room for success provided obstacles are overcome, and they are only to be overcome at the price of energy and hard work.

If Luther's letter of October 31, 1517, to Archbishop Albrecht is truly important, and it is, then it is one of the oddities of literary history that it is the postscript of this letter that has made it so illustrious, historical and significant. In fact, it is the postscript whose anniversary is marked this year. The letter concludes with this formula:

I pray that you may accept this humble but faithful admonition graciously as ruler and bishop, even as I submit it with a faithful and devoted heart. For I, too, am one of you sheep. The Lord guard and guide you forever. Amen.[15]

Then, almost as an afterthought the words appear:

If you, Reverend Father, so desire, you might look at the enclosed set of propositions to recognize how indefinite the concept of indulgences is, even though the indulgence preachers consider it altogether certain.[16]

"The enclosed set of propositions" is known to us as "the ninety-five theses of Doctor Martin Luther." It is this celebrated collection of themes or paradoxes that spiraled the religious hurricane that swept through Europe as the Protestant Reformation. Luther may have nailed these theses to the door of the Schlosskirche in Wittenberg, as tradition alleges; but he certainly mailed them to the archbishop as his own letter attests. Whether he nailed them or mailed them, he certainly "posted" them.[17]

The ninety-five theses of Luther do not technically represent the beginning of the Reformation as history knows it. They are a protest against public abuse and have become a symbol of defiance of authority. But their symbolic value has often been misunderstood; in no sense were these theses originally intended to turn the Church upside down and inside out. History sees in them a symbol of religious division and ecclesiastical schism; for, as the full significance of the Lutheran affair in the context of the Church became apparent, Christendom began to fall apart. Men separated from one another; distinct communities formed; *communicatio in sacris*—common prayer and worship—became mortally forbidden. All men took sides on the great question, each for his own good or poor reason. Rarely were the academic issues really clear, the religious consequences truly manifest, and the theological questions properly formulated. This age was an age of religious passion and conviction joined to theological hardheadedness and temper—powerful and dangerous combinations of attitudes.

The Lutheran theses are the small foyer that leads into a much larger, more spacious ambit where activity, both religious and political, was to take place. The theses, as we know and study them today, were not intended originally for popular gossip, dispute, and wrangling. Of this Luther wrote:

> It is a mystery to me how my theses . . . were spread to so many places. They were meant exclusively for our academic circle here. This is shown by the fact that they were written in such language that the common people could hardly understand them. They are propositions for debate, not dogmatic definitions, and they use academic categories. . . .[18]

The sudden popularity of his theses may have come as a sudden surprise to Luther; but it might well illustrate what Wilhelm Dilthey meant, when he wrote: "He [Luther] had an extraordinary talent for sensing the needs of the time and for unifying its active thought."[19]

The theses of Luther emerged in the religious context of the early sixteenth century. The old Church needed renewal and reform on all levels—morals, theology, spirituality, liturgy and structure.[20] In fact, the question of Church reform was a burning question even a century before Luther. As early as the Council of Constance (1414–18) the expression *Reformatio ecclesiae in capite et in membris* was voiced on all sides. The issue of reform was not totally neglected; but it could not be totally handled. The history of the period is filled with futile attempts on the part of good, discerning, capable, even saintly men, to reform the Church. But something more effective than purely individual and personal concern was needed.

Giles of Viterbo (1469–1532) sensed the disaster, and described it to the Fathers of the Fifth Lateran Council (1512–17) at their opening session on May 3, 1512:

> I see, yes I see that, unless by this Council or by some other means we place a limit on our morals, unless we force our greedy desire for human things, the source of evils, to yield to the love of divine things, it is all over with Christendom, all over with religion, even all over with those very resources which our fathers acquired by their greater service of God, but which we are about to lose because of our neglect.[21]

In concluding he made a sincere plea to the Fathers "to reform the Church . . . and to curb their unbridled living which afflicts the heart of the Church with very great wounds." Within a matter of months after the close of this Council, Luther was engaged in correcting the indulgence abuses of Germany.

In the opening decades of the sixteenth century the Western world had reached a point of extreme tension which weighed heavily on the old structures and bent them acutely. A newness of life, of *manière d'être*, was developing; new forms of science, art and literature were being created; a new mind was emerging and beginning to think its own thoughts in its own way. The art of printing from movable type had been perfected by Johannes Gutenberg (ca. 1396–1468); the New World was discovered in 1492; Nicolas Copernicus (1473–

1543) had devised a revolutionary conception of the universe. The medieval was burning out, and from its ashes the modern world was arising that would give birth to men of different values, works, ambitions, thoughts and methods. The cathedral at Strasburg is a symbol of the old and the new. The old order commenced this sacred building and brought it almost to completion. It remains unfinished, for the divided Christian community could no longer realize it as a common religious enterprise. To this day the solitary spire of the Strasburg cathedral remains a symbol of the changing Christian life of Europe—partly united, partly divided, partly incomplete with work left over to be finished one day.

The man of the sixteenth century took religion seriously—too seriously, perhaps, for after all religion as a moral virtue "stat in medio." It stands "in the middle" and avoids extremes—laxism and fanaticism. Before long, pope and emperor, bishop and prince, town and gown, artisan and tradesman had become theologians, disputants and partisans. And, of course, the humanists of the day had to have their say, and occasionally the universities came to life long enough to give advice to the disputants. Europe had become the arena of a great religious debating society in which very few rules of courtesy were observed. And the fact that the sixteenth century brought the art of name-calling to its perfection did not help to ease the tense atmosphere that then prevailed.

One has the impression that the men of that day believed that names hurt more than "sticks and stones that break bones." At least that is the way they acted and spoke. There was a battle of bitter words that poured out like a torrent. Everyone was right, and everyone was wrong. We politely call this verbal exchange "the confessional polemic"; actually it was a confessional war. Before long, words yielded to bloodshed, persuasion to physical violence. The first phase of the Reformation was a hard century. Perhaps never before or since did the flames of Christian charity burn so low. It is a tragedy that so many of the men of this period in their zeal to discover the meaning of Christian life forgot how to live it. The bitterness which "the great split" engendered is epitomized by the last words of Bl. Margaret Clitherow (d. 1586) to the ministers who wished to pray with her before her martyrdom: "I will not pray with you," she said, "nor shall you pray with me; neither will I say Amen to your prayers, nor shall you to mine."[22]

As the polemic developed sides were taken to the right or to the left; few stood in the middle of the road, at least for long. Emperor Charles V regarded Luther with the utmost scorn. "That fellow," he said, "will never make a heretic of me." Then he added later:

> It is certain that a single monk errs in his opinion which is against what all of Christendom has held for over a thousand years to the present. According to his opinion all of Christendom has always been in error. To settle this matter I am therefore determined to use all my dominions and possessions, my friends, my body, my blood, my life and my soul. . . . I will have no more to do with him. . . . I will proceed against him as a notorious heretic. . . .[23]

Henry VIII (1491–1547) was equally adamant against Luther and his "novel" Lutheranism, and heaped bitter scorn upon the friar and his theology, in which he saw a subversion of the whole structure of Christendom.[24]

But what is most surprising is the attitude of Thomas More (1478–1535) and Desiderius Erasmus (ca. 1466–1536), two of the outstanding humanists of the day, both well acquainted with the corruption and decadence of contemporary ecclesiastical and monastic life. After all, they had both lived through the pontificates of Alexander VI (1492–1503) and Julius II (1503–13). Logically they should have gone over totally to the reform movement. Why adhere to a religious cause that seemed utterly lost and worth forsaking? The comments of St. Thomas More on Luther may be unworthy of a saint, but they make his position clear and pointed. He wrote:

> Luther handles his subject matter in such a way that it is quite clear that he dreams of some absurd kind of immortality. He lives, moves and has his very being in the titillating excitement of this little glory; he imagines that after some thousands of years men, looking back, will speak of a certain rascal who lived once upon a time named Luther, who surpassed demons in impiety . . . overcame magpies in garrulity, procurers in depravity, prostitutes in obscenity and fools in foolishness! . . . This truly absurd

variety of heretic, this offscouring of impiety, crime and filth is called Lutheran.[25]

He further described Luther as "a blockhead character . . . a vain rascal . . . and a mind crazed by a lust for glory." I mention this here not to be offensive, but rather in a picturesque way to illustrate the theme of this essay—that the Roman Catholic world, even to the point of differing with its saints, has changed its evaluation of Luther and Lutheranism, and, therefore, of Protestantism generally.

Erasmus—humanist, religious and Catholic—was expert par excellence on abuses in the Church. No ecclesiastic of his day wrote as strongly, bitterly, and independently on corruption, fraud, superstition and inauthenticity of any and every kind no matter where it was to be found. He even authored the *Encomium Moriae* as a biting satire on ecclesiastical abuse. For a time he stood in the middle of the road, looked both to the right and to the left, and did not seem to care for what he saw. Yet he wrote in 1522: "Neither death nor life shall draw me from the communion of the Catholic Church." And in the *Hyperaspistes* in 1526 he wrote again:

> I have never been an apostate from the Catholic Church. I know that in this Church, which you call the Papist Church, there are many who displease me, but such I also see in your Church. One bears more easily the evils to which one is accustomed. Therefore I bear with this Church, until I shall see a better, and it cannot help bearing with me, until I shall myself be better. . . .[26]

Erasmus could be terribly hard in his pronouncements on this Church to which he adhered. He was never considered "a safe man"; he was too outspoken on too many sensitive areas. But he could be equally stern with the Reformers and their accomplishments. Thus he wrote of the Protestant renewal of his day:

> Just look at the Evangelical people, have they become any better? Do they yield less to luxury, lust and greed? Show me a man whom that Gospel has changed from a toper to a temperate man, from a brute to a gentle creature. . . . I will show you many who have become even worse than they were.[27]

Thus the polemic, bitter and sharp, developed. On their side the Protestants had equally clever and biting things to say. It was a battle of words and deeds opening a precipitous chasm that made dialogue difficult, understanding prejudiced, and love impossible.

The polemic, which commenced in the sixteenth century, has continued down the years, down even to the twentieth century. When Heinrich Seuse Denifle (1844–1905) published in 1904 his *Luther und Luthertum in der ersten Entwicklung*, the scholarly world was shocked. For here the explanation of Luther's revolt was traced to his uncontrollable sensuality, and no detail was spared in telling it. "This book," remarked Denifle, "is not intended for the young. Such is the real Luther," and the preface concludes: "May God open the eyes of the Protestants to Luther's character and bring them back to the Catholic Church."[28] This was a high point in the polemic because Denifle was a scholar of repute who allowed himself to drift from objectivity in his scientific judgment. The unfortunate book has done as much harm to Catholics as to Protestants.

One last document—the encyclical of St. Pius X, *Editae saepe* (May 26, 1910)—is worth citing to illustrate the burden that the Catholic reappraisal of Luther and the Reformation has to bear. Here the pope writes of the Protestants of the days of St. Charles Borromeo (1538–84):

> There arose proud and arrogant men, enemies of the Cross of Christ . . . earthly minded men whose God is their belly. These . . . multiplied disorders, giving themselves and others unbridled license; they spurned the authorized guidance of the Church to follow the most corrupt of passions, principles and persons. . . .[29]

These specimens I present here with reluctance; but yet with a certain joy and hope in the realization that the Catholic Church is trying now, in these days of ecumenism, to overcome the dark inspirations of her past history, not by words alone but by deeds.

Since 1517 the Christian Church has changed her ways and means, her outlook, her tastes and preferences. If she has not become more Christian, she has certainly become more civil and more than tolerant. The ecumenical movement of our day is a testimonial to the ultimate victory of the charity of Jesus Christ over all Christian issues in this world. How astonishing it would strike our forefathers, Pope Leo X, Archbishop Albrecht of Mainz, and Doctor Johannes Eck of Ingolstadt, to learn that one day Catholics and Lutherans would sit down together in peace and friendship to mark the anniversary of the ninety-five theses! How unbelievable it would seem to Martin Luther, to Philip Melanchthon and Andreas Carlstadt to learn that one day a saintly man, the late Pope John XXIII, would sit on the throne of St. Peter and there receive the honor, respect and friendship of the entire Christian world both Catholic and Protestant! And who would have thought after the Council of Trent with its divisive spirit that Protestants would be invited to attend a Catholic ecumenical council in Rome, and that they would be present as gracious guests and keen observers? And, last of all, would any sixteenth-century churchman ever have envisioned a day when the two confessions would be able goodnaturedly to laugh at one another's foibles rather than drawing swords? Must not considerations such as these make us humble face to face with the working out of salvation history?

All this means that we Christians are growing up, coming of age, maturing in a truly human way. The development of the past four hundred and fifty years—despite the scandals and atrocities that have marked them (often in the name of Christ)—represents the resilience of Christianity to change, adaptation and transformation; but above all it suggests the eternal endurance of the Christian Gospel. For what save this holy testament holds us all together as a community of true believers in Christ? It is this consideration that once and for all should silence the pseudo-prophets of doom, despair, separation and division. For the Lord's petition that we all be one is still operative. The fascination of "the one Church of Christ" holds us together in its grip. We cannot bypass it, ignore or overlook it. Even after centuries the mystique of Church unity is still with us. This is what the early Christian martyrs may have meant when they spoke of the *mysterium simplicitatis*—"the mystery of simplicity."

Between Protestantism and Catholicism there is fundamentally a mysterious analogy in which the similarities are greater than the dissimilarities. Both have sprung from the great medieval Church, the ultimate mother of all Christian churches; both claim the Gospel as their primordial foundation; both are concerned with man, his renovation and salvation, and both reverence and confess the one crucified and risen Lord as the Alpha and Omega of all. In four and one-half centuries the two Christian communities have changed. The Evangelical more quickly and drastically; the Catholic more slowly and sparingly. The former, for example, is less prone to cling to the words of Luther; the latter is less enamored with the spirit of Trent. Perhaps both will suffer for the manner in which they have changed; the one for its verve, the other for its immobility. The Christian Church is a living Church; it grows and changes—not by leaps and bounds, neither by fits and starts, but according to its own inner vital principle and ethos.

Catholic theology has been repudiated by Protestants, at times by way of caricature, at times out of sheer indifference, but at times after prolonged study. Anyone who knows the religious history of the fourteenth and fifteenth centuries knows that abuses had crept into traditional Christianity, and by "abuse" here I do not mean immorality in the narrow sense of the word. I mean, rather, that the Church by reason of her vastness, her antiquity, her conservatism, her power and position in medieval Christendom—especially by reason of the secular cares and concerns which she either assumed or which were thrust upon her—neglected certain fundamental aspects of the development of Christian life. The reproach is not so much against the Church for what she did as against the Church for what she did not do. I would say that the late medieval Church failed in apostolate more by passive neglect than by active abuse. The Church of God is the Church of Christ; it is the church of men, and, after all, men are men. They are never angels and they are rarely saints.

The Catholic regard for good works, their value and their place in Christian life was truly a sore point with the Reformers. In the course of the late medieval period a religious abuse had crept into Catholic practice: the idea, namely, that certain human works of their own value lead on to eternal salvation; these good works were too often tied up with indulgences, and indulgences too often were represen-

ted as part of "the mechanics of salvation." The "negotium indul-
gentiarum"—the indulgence business—was not good; it represented
an abuse of decadent theology, which Josef Lortz has described this
way:

> Within the Roman Catholic Church, from the fourteenth century on, an
> ever-increasing theological uncertainty had made itself felt, so that by the
> end of the Middle Ages the whole situation was characterized by a great
> deal of confusion in theological matters.[30]

Late medieval theology may have been uncertain; but it was not
corrupt. But theology as taught and theology as lived often deviate;
religion as a virtue is not always regulated by theology as a science.
It is one thing to point to tomes of orthodox theology, another to the
unorthodox lives of men. The comprehension of good works and
their connection with salvation illustrates this *theologische Unklarheit*
—"theological uncertainty"—of the eve of the Reformation.

The indulgence practice was an abuse which could and should have
been corrected by ecclesiastical authority. It was not, at least not at
once. Catholic theologians have often caricatured the Protestant
concept of good works this way: "It is good to live as a Protestant,
because you do not have to do good works to be saved; it is better to
die as a Catholic because your good works go to heaven with you."
There is need of truth and objectivity here. Catholic doctrine in its
pure form never taught that the kingdom of God could be simply
bought by good works; Protestants never simply repudiated good
works as part of Christian living. But neverthelss there is behind this
talk a much broader issue which is of more than historical interest.

The Catholic theology of good works takes its inspiration from
Scripture, from *loci* such as the twenty-fifth chapter of Matthew's
Gospel, where the circumstances of the final judgment of mankind are
described. Here the Lord grants eternal life to those who have done
good for their fellow men, while he repudiates those who have failed
to assist their neighbor in his need. For the Catholic this Gospel theme
is good works in the context of eternal life. From these and other
texts he constructs his concept of good works and eternal merit. The
underlying presumption is that the "do-gooder," when he does good

with charity, is God's friend, and that God will not overlook "the here and now" goodness of His friends. There is no question either of buying, earning, or meriting eternal salvation sheerly by human work, however good and perfect it may be. This brief description is necessarily oversimplified; it is only intended to indicate a thought pattern rather than a qualified theological statement, but it brings out a humanistic aspect of the Catholic doctrine of good works, a doctrine unfortunately corroded in the ebb and flow of history, and not properly posed in the late Middle Ages.[31]

The Catholic doctrine of good works has profound humanistic implications. First of all, it is based on the belief that man, even though fallen, is still capable of doing natural good; his fallen human nature is not totally and intrinsically vitiated and corrupt. That human life in itself has a value is a basic optimism that the Fathers of Trent and the Tridentine Church were not ready to relinquish. Second, the Catholic doctrine of good works, properly understood, exalts human life as such, and the totality of all the good that man accomplishes here and now, in the order of faith and history. Every good work, performed by man as a faithful friend of God, is of eternal value and merit. Human accomplishment here below is not of passing significance; it is more than ripe fruit falling in its fullness from a good tree. It merits God's consideration for all eternity. The sixth session (January 13, 1547) of Trent forms a veritable act of confidence in the goodness of man and his accomplishment.

In the popular fiction of history the problematic of the Reformation is too often described as a great protest against relics, saints, Mariolatry and the like, and against legalism and its law and lawyers, against "the pomp and circumstance" of the medieval Church. There is an element of truth in all this; but most of these abuses are secondary to a much broader, more decisive issue, the issue on which all hangs and has hung for centuries wherever there has been question of Protestant and Catholic dialogue. In the days of the Arian controversy the central question was: "What do you think of Jesus? Whose Son is he?" Since the Reformation one has asked: "What do you think of the Church? What is she? Where is she?" The question is important; it is difficult, and it is still sensitive. After all, its answer divides us all into Evangelical and Catholic Christians. It is the question which, when acceptably answered, will one day close the circle of history and bring us all together as one believing and worshiping community.[32]

Luther reacted more against the structure of the Church than against the Church itself; he resented many of its forms and attitudes, its method and its technique. The unfortunate circumstances which overtook him from the beginning involved him in legal structure; against this and all that it represented he fought to the bitter end. Theology, his own well-thought-out concept of Christianity, shaped him into a protester, a dissenter and a reformer. The Council of Trent had assembled on December 13, 1545, and before it had reached its celebrated fourth session Luther had died. At his obsequies on February 22, 1546, Johann Bugenhagen spoke of his old friend in these moving words:

> . . . he was without doubt the angel of which the Apocalypse speaks in Chapter XIV: "And I saw an angel flying through the midst of heaven, who had an eternal gospel to preach," . . . the angel who says: "Fear God, and give glory to Him!" These are the two articles of the teaching of Martin Luther, the law and the Gospel, by which the whole Scripture is opened and Christ made known as our righteousness and eternal life.[33]

Luther died, but the Church lives on, and Bugenhagen may well have reduced "the two articles . . . the law and the Gospel" to one article—the evangelical Church of Christ on earth.

Luther left as a heritage an understanding of the Christian Church which to this day has remained an obstacle to Catholics in their quest of unity. In many points it may coincide with the Roman Church; but deeply, essentially, and meaningfully the two are at variance in their approach to God through the Church. Two different views of Christianity are at issue here, two different ways of conceiving salvation, two different mentalities—but not so very different as to be hostile, opposed and contentious. To be different only means not to be the same; but it does not import a dialectic that leads to violence or to an impossible impasse. We Christians of this day and age have come to an appreciation of religious differences, to understand and sympathize with them, to leave snobbery aside and to be even more than tolerant. The day may come and may not be far off when the religious thought of Martin Luther will be more congenial to the Catholic than to the Evangelical community. The genius of subsequent generations to resolve and compound differences is beyond our imaginations.

What really and essentially is Roman Catholicism? What are the heart and soul of this Church which has been a fundamental part of the Western world for more than a thousand years and which currently embraces a half-billion members in all corners of the globe? I do not really know; for in Catholic theology the Church is presented as a mystery—the mystery of Christ's continuing presence in this world among His own and others, healing, redeeming and saving them. I call the Church a mystery—a religious truth which cannot be fully comprehended by men—not to avoid a difficult theological question, but rather because there are other aspects of the Church which pertain more closely to the theme of this essay and which are more concretely tangible.

First of all, Roman Catholicism is a social religion, not merely a society, a *Gemeinde* or a *Gemeinschaft*, as Luther put it.[34] It is a religious reality of the social order, of the order of men and their concerns, which envisions and demands that, while human beings ultimately depend on God through faith and charity, they also depend on one another. In the historical and social order the distribution of the fruits of redemption is the cooperative work of man. No Catholic baptizes himself; no Catholic forgives his own sins; no Catholic preaches the Gospel to himself; no Catholic worships alone in his liturgy; no Catholic anoints himself as death approaches. Instinctively the Roman Catholic turns to his fellow man as to God's instrument and *from* him and *through* him receives "the universal medicine" of salvation as St. Augustine put it. This is not a novel idea. As God redeemed the world through the humanity of Christ the man, Christ the man continues to redeem men through the humanity of other men. In this context Wilhelm Dilthey's evaluation of medieval Christianity as "a supersensual regimental proceeding" seems meaningless.[35] Even at its lowest level the Church of the

Middle Ages knew and believed that men save men in this world through the merits of Jesus Christ, the Man-God.

The Catholic dialogue with God is essentially "We-Thou," not "I-Thou." As a member of the ecclesiastical community, no Catholic stands alone face to face with God. The Church is always with him. He finds it congenial and connatural to live and pray as part of a vast worshipping and believing community which through its adherence to its own traditions imparts a unique vision of life both here below and there above. It is in this sense that the Catholic repudiates pure individualism in any and every form, individualism that deviates from and distorts the soul and body of Christ which is the Church on earth.

Paolo Sarpi (1552–1623) was convinced that the Council of Trent is the great dividing line between Protestantism and Catholicism, the watershed between Rome and Wittenberg, between the old and the new. After Trent, "the great Iliade of our age," as he called it, the Western world knew two separate, distinct Christian communities. His judgment is questionable, but its answer exceeds the scope of this essay. The Tridentine Fathers failed in many respects, but not in all respects. They failed to redefine for the Catholic world what the Church is, what her authority means, how both are instruments to serve men unto salvation, and how a meaningless Church anarchy results from the negation of authority. Trent also failed to give the Church a new structure that would make it more adaptable to the new world which was then being formed and opened. And though the council never condemned a single reformer by name and did attempt in one form or another to bring the reformers to the council,[36] it froze the Church into certain rigid attitudes that tended to withdraw her more and more into herself. The post-Tridentine Church developed a horror of theological divergence of opinion that made meaningful relations between the different Christian communities impossible. But this issue, however bitter it may be, must be faced fully. If the post-Tridentine Catholics were intransigent, the pre-Tridentine Protestants were equally so in their own righteous way. Rarely in history is the responsibility for failure all in one direction.

The Fathers of Trent were men of their day; some were scholars, some were saints, some were enigmatic, difficult characters, creatures of another age. Many of them were angry men, men who resented Luther in whom they saw the man who had divided and broken up what they considered to be "the one family of Christ"—Christendom. This is the way they thought and spoke. Some of them understood Luther; most did not. It is easy for us to criticize these Fathers of Trent because none of them is on hand to explain and defend himself. And how very easy it is to moralize and pontificate over the rectitude or turpitude of our forefathers who lived centuries ago and whose bones have long since turned to dust.

But there is one insight from the Council of Trent that helps to summarize what this essay intends apropos of the Catholic reevaluation of the past four hundred and fifty years. In the very last session of the Council, on December 4, 1563, Bishop Hieronymus Ragazonus preached to the Fathers gathered together for the last time. He explicated the significance of the Council and developed the history of the past eighteen years of conciliar debate. When he adverted to the Protestants and their absence from the Council he spoke these sad words:

> Oh, that those for whose sake this voyage was chiefly undertaken had decided to board it with us; that those who caused us to take up this work in hand had participated in the erection of this edifice! Then indeed we would now have reason for greater rejoicing. But it is certainly not through our fault that it so happened. For that reason we chose this city [Trent], situated at the entrance to Germany, situated almost at the thresholds of their homes . . . for a long time we awaited them and never did we cease to exhort them and plead with them to come here and learn the truth. . . .[37]

The historical fact is that the Protestants of that day did not go to Trent "to learn the truth"; but neither are the Catholics of this day waiting, pleading, and exhorting the Protestants "to come to us." We do want to meet somewhere, whether high in the Alps, on the plains of Missouri, in a city skyscraper, or on a university campus; when we meet, we must be open and ready "with the charity of truth" to talk about important things, to discuss and debate "the" issues which both divide and unite us, to share and finally to learn the truth together. The contemporary Catholic invitation to Protestants is not, therefore, Tridentine. It derives largely from the ecumenical spirit of the Second Vatican Council, and herein is to be found ultimately the Catholic reappraisal of the Reformation. When we meet together as Christians, it will be our chief consolation to know that wherever some faithful are gathered together in the name of the Lord, He will be in our midst. Inevitably the sad polemic of the past four hundred and fifty years will terminate one day in a joyous victory of Christ Jesus whose name we all honor and confess with reverence.

NOTES

1. Cf. for the text of this letter Hans J. Hillerbrand, *The Reformation* (New York, 1964), pp. 49–51.

2. For example, by 1517 Luther had already prepared important commentaries on the Psalms and the Epistle to the Galatians. These were outgrowths of his university lectures.

3. Cf. H. J. Hillerbrand, *op. cit.*, p. 22.

4. For example, he refers to himself as "the scum of the earth" who is making bold to address the great archbishop.

5. Cf. H. J. Hillerbrand, *op. cit.*, pp. 49–50.

6. Cf. *ibid.*, p. 50.

7. Cf. *ibid.*

8. Cf. R. E. McNally, s.j., "The Ninety-five Theses of Martin Luther: 1517–1967," *Theological Studies* 28 (1967), 439–80, for a discussion of the involved legal process growing out of Luther's denunciation of the indulgence abuse.

9. In these terms Charles V described himself to the princes assembled at the Diet of Worms (April 19, 1521).

10. Cf. R. H. Bainton, *Here I Stand: A Life of Martin Luther* (New York, 1950), pp. 148–49.

11. Cf. *ibid.*, p. 149.

12. Cf. R. E. McNally, s.j., *op. cit.*, p. 478. It was not until November 9, 1518, "that the chancery of Pope Leo X published the Bull *Cum postquam*, which aimed at correcting both the theological and the pastoral abuses connected with the indulgence preaching."

13. Cf. J. Wicks, s.j., "Martin Luther's Treatise on Indulgences," *Theological*

Studies 28 (1967), 461, esp., 482: "... the treatise depicts in orderly and succinct fashion Luther's understanding of indulgences in 1517 and reveals his conception of their limited role in Christian living. The treatise gives us the theological standpoint on which Luther based his intervention, and it shows in miniature the rich Augustinian spirituality of penance and the progress that he had forged in his early works."

14. Cf. *Luther's Works* 48, *Letters* 1, edit., and trans., by G. G. Krodel (Philadelphia, 1963), 341: Luther (Dec. 1, 1521) at Wartburg to Cardinal Albrecht of Mainz.

15. Cf. H. Hillerbrand, *op. cit.*, p. 51.

16. Cf. *ibid.*

17. See J.Wicks, S.J., *op. cit.*, p. 482, n. 1, and L. Spitz, "Current Accents in Luther Study: 1960–67," *Theological Studies* 28 (1967), 570, n. 11, for a summary of the recent literature on the method by which Luther "posted" his theses.

18. Cf. H. Hillerbrand, *op. cit.*, p. 53. Luther wrote these lines (May 30, 1518) in his *Resolutions* dedicated to Pope Leo X.

19. Cited from his *Auffassung und Analyse des Menschen im 15. und 16. Jahrhundert*, translated by Edna Spitz in *The Reformation*, edit. L.W. Spitz (Boston, 1962), p. 11.

20. Cf. R. E. McNally, S.J., *The Unreformed Church* (New York, 1965).

21. For this reference to Giles of Viterbo and the translation of his sermon I am indebted with gratitude to Prof. John C. Olin. Cf. also J. W. O'Malley, S.J., "Giles of Viterbo: A Reformer's Thought on Renaissance Rome," *Renaissance Quarterly* 20 (1967), 1–11.

22. Cf. R. E. McNally, S.J., *The Reform of the Church* (New York, 1963), pp. 104–05, n. 4. Mary Claridge, *Margaret Clitherow* (New York, 1966), p. 174.

23. Cf. H. J. Hillerbrand, *op. cit.*, p. 94: "The morning after Luther's second appearance Emperor Charles V assembled the rulers and stated his own position."

24. His work, the *Assertio Septem Sacramentorum* (1521), was directed against Martin Luther and won for him from Pope Leo X the celebrated title "Defender of the Faith."

25. Cf. G. J. Donnelly, *A Translation of St. Thomas More's Responsio ad Lutherum* (Washington, 1962), pp. 256–59.

26. Cited from J. Huizinga, *Erasmus and the Age of Reformation* (New York, 1957), p. 165.

27. Cf. *ibid.*, p. 177.

28. For this and the following reference I am indebted to the Rev. James J. Hennesey, S.J., *The Origins and Development of the Görres Society, 1876–1916* (unpublished dissertation, The Catholic University of America, 1960), p. 116.

29. Cf. *ibid.*, p. 96.

30. Cf. J. Lortz, *The Reformation: a Problem for Today* (Westminster, Md., 1964), p. 42.

31. Cf. H. J. Schroeder, O.P., *Canons and Decrees of the Council of Trent* (St. Louis, 1941), pp. 29–46, where the Sixth Session of Trent clarifies the gratuity of justification.

32. Cf. H. Jedin, "Ist das Konzil von Trient ein Hindernis der Wiedervereinigung?" *Ephemerides theologicae Lovanienses* 38 (1962), 849, where he significantly remarks: "In the forty years that I have studied reformation history I have formed the conviction (which becomes ever stronger) that the deepest impasse, which separates Catholics and Protestants, is the doctrine of neither justification nor salvation, but ecclesiology" (my translation).

33. Cited from W. Pauck, *The Heritage of the Reformation* (Glencoe, 1961), p. 19.

34. Cf. *ibid.*, pp. 32ff., for a very penetrating study of "Luther's Conception of the Church."

35. Cf. *The Reformation* (cited in n. 19 *supra*), p. 12.

36. Cf. R. E. McNally, S.J., "The Council of Trent and the German Protestants," *Theological Studies* 25 (1964), 1–22.

37. Cf. H. J. Schroeder, O.P., *op. cit.*, p. 259.

3

The "Catholic" Luther

WILHELM PAUCK

IT IS NO EXAGGERATION to say that the interpretation of Martin Luther's person and work has been subject to greater changes than is usual in the evaluation of the accomplishments of influential or representative men. This is due to many complicated factors. The sources about his life and career, indeed, his own voluminous writings and utterances, are so rich and many-sided that they can be interpreted in many ways. They are also full of so many contradictions that they lend themselves to varied explanations. It is an amazing fact that the only complete historical-critical edition of his works which was begun in 1883, the year of the 400th anniversary of his birth, is still not fully completed, and that, despite the availability of many excellent and suggestive studies of his life and thought, neither historians nor theologians have as yet produced either a definitive biographical description of his life or a complete historical analysis of his thought. The picture which his own Protestant descendants and successors have drawn of him has changed with the times, even among those who are named after him.

Only Roman Catholics, so it seems, have entertained a consistent view of him. It is understandable that the condemnation pronounced against him on January 3, 1521, by Pope Leo X has determined this judgment throughout the years. Moreover, it has been given a special content and color by the first biography of Luther published by a Roman Catholic, namely that of Johannes Cochlaeus, first printed in 1549 under the title *Commentaria de actis et scriptis M. Lutheri*. As the modern (Roman Catholic) historian Adolf Herte has shown in a large and detailed work comprising three volumes, this first biography, written in the spirit of detestation and hatred, has exercised a continuous formative impact upon the picture which Roman Catholics have held of Luther, down to the larger scholarly biographies of Denifle and Grisar and the judgments of modern popes and churchmen. Luther is depicted as a heretic who, as an innovator and rebel, motivated by sick and evil desires, inaugurated the Protestant "Revolt." But now this view is undergoing a radical change. Roman Catholic scholars have begun to treat Luther as a "*homo religiosus*." They make an effort to understand and appreciate his faith as they evaluate his thoughts and actions in the light of the conditions prevailing in the Roman Church from which they arose.

The decisive new work is that of Joseph Lortz, first published in 1939 in two volumes and since then re-issued in several new editions under the title: "The Reformation in Germany." The author is an irenic and ecumenically minded interpreter of the Reformation. He is fully acquainted with the intensive modern research in the beginnings of Protestantism, and he endeavors to draw an objective picture of the events which led to the breakup of the medieval church. He finds it possible to write of Luther in a spirit of sympathy and admiration. Not only in his chief work but also in smaller articles and treatises he expresses himself again and again in an astonishingly positive way about Luther's genius. In an analysis of Luther's intellectual character which he contributed to the *Festschrift* for H. Jedin (another Roman Catholic Reformation historian of the new school whose outlook is similar to that of Lortz but somewhat less personal and more objective), he writes:

> As one tries to depict Luther, one becomes aware of the vast distance between what he was in himself and what one wants to say about him. Again and again one feels oneself constrained simply to quote him in order to let him be himself in his wonderful way of letting himself go and of digging indefatigably into all kinds of things: in the immense force and the almost immeasurable height, breadth, and depth of his preaching; in the amazing vitality and fullness of his task as a reformer who was taken hold of by the spirit of the word of Scripture——and all this despite innumerable repetitions. . . . Then again one finds that this way of [Luther's] is bound (and often disturbed) by an attitude that is instinctively wholly uncritical,

violent, and misleading and yet again and again revealing of a naïveté which is capable of expressing itself in unforgettably charming words.[1]

No wonder that the man who wrote this and whose views found an astonishingly friendly echo among his fellow-Catholics was also able to write:

> Today, so it seems to me, it is no longer settled who is better prepared for a really adequate understanding of Luther: the Evangelical or the Catholic scholar![2]

Then he goes on to remark:

> (1) We Catholics have gradually come to realize the Christian, indeed the Catholic richness of Luther's thought and we are deeply impressed by this; (2) we have come to realize also how greatly Roman Catholicism is responsible for Luther's expulsion from the church with the result that the church became divided; (3) we are strongly moved by the desire to bring home to the Catholic Church all the great and positive substance of Luther's thought.

This remarkably favorable judgment about Luther does not dispense Professor Lortz from the necessity of explaining how it happened that Luther was declared a heretic or whether Luther was a heretic. Lortz shows that the leaders of the church lacked the ability to assess properly the importance of Luther's thought and action but he never even intimates that he feels that Luther was unjustly condemned. On the contrary, he, too, is convinced that Luther was a heretic and he explains this by a noteworthy two-fold argument. In the first place, he maintains that Luther was educated in a theological school which was no longer fully Catholic. His Occamist teachers taught him an understanding of the gospel and the church which was un-balanced. In the course of his own development as a theologian and churchman, Luther was led to protest against this Catholicism but he did not realize that there was a better, truer Catholicism in the church and that, because of his own upbringing, he was incapable of correcting his views in the proper way. From here Lortz goes on to attribute to Luther a one-sidedness which ultimately forced him outside the orbit of the Catholic Church. He writes:

The Christian spirit can be rightly interpreted only if objective events are seen in correlation with subjective attitudes. The wholeness of Christianity is not safeguarded unless these two elements are connected with one another. But this must be done in such a way that the inner attitudes of man are made to appear as less important than the objective power and the objective life of the mystical body of Christ. Yet it is undeniable that for man the decisive factor in this relationship is . . . the better, inward righteousness of a new heart and conscience. Whenever this obligation is taken singly by itself, the Protestant attitude is produced . . . for an exaggeration of personal religious earnestness signifies the danger of heresy.[3]

In this light, Lortz sees Luther. He attributes to him an exaggerated concern for personal religiousness which caused him to deny and to revolt against the primacy of the divine as it objectively confronts man in the authoritative priestly and sacramental institutions of the church. To be sure, he recognizes that Luther did not intend to "empty" Christianity of its objective source of power, and he acknowledges that Luther's thinking was always based on the conviction that his conscience was held captive by the word of God, as Luther put it in his famous speech at Worms. But he feels that he must judge that Luther failed to comprehend fully what was given to him in the objectivity of Scripture. Lortz sums up his views as follows:

> With all his powers, Luther seeks only the one God and he desires to be wholly subject to him. Having found God in the word of the Bible, he submits to the authority of the word . . . yet, from the beginning, his submissiveness is sometimes totally different from the simple receptiveness of the plain Christian. It is at all times an act of appropriation by Luther, the seeker, the fighter, the gigantic wrestler. And this is the decisive point: He who wishes to surrender unconditionally to God's word, never succeeds fully in being a listener. In the roots of his being, Luther is inclined toward subjectiveness.[4]

Professor Lortz is prepared to admit that Luther wished to be, and indeed was, a servant of the word, but he feels that he was such a servant "in a very personal sense." By absolutizing and isolating the word, he caused religious objectivism to become an illusion, for a religious objectivism (one can also say: absolutism) is impossible unless it is assured again and again by an infallible, living, teaching office.[5] "Relying upon his own individual knowledge and interpretation of the Bible, he sovereignly passed by the church."[6] Thus he became inwardly separated from true Catholicism long before he was excommunicated, and, insofar as he persisted in this conviction throughout his life, he remained an outsider.

The upshot of Professor Lortz's views appears to be that, although there is much in Luther that Roman Catholics should absorb, he was not really a good Catholic because he was too one-sided in his subjectivism.

It is interesting to consider in this connection the studies of one of Lortz's students, Professor Erwin Iserloh, who has quickly become an eminent Luther scholar. In recent years, he has focused his attention on the beginnings of the Reformation and particularly on the publication of the 95 theses.

In a monograph published under the title *Luther zwischen Reform und Reformation* (Münster, 1966), he has convincingly shown that Luther did not tack his theses on the door of the castle church in Wittenberg on the eve of All Saints' Day in 1517. The originator of this story, which generations of Protestants have believed to be symbolical both of Luther's resoluteness and of the spirit of the Reformation, was Philip Melanchthon. In 1546, shortly after Luther's death, he wrote a brief biography of his friend and published it in the form of a preface to the second volume of Luther's Latin works. Its accuracy was never doubted by anyone—until, a few years ago, modern historians became aware of the fact that Luther, who had a tendency to speak freely about his career and who, in his later years, loved to reminisce, never mentioned the incident. Moreover, there are no other contemporary sources which support the old story.

All this does not seem to be very important. But, nevertheless, there are significant implications in this for an interpretation of Luther's personality and character in relation to the beginning of the Reformation.

What can be established from the sources is that on October 31, 1517, Luther addressed letters to his ecclesiastical superiors, the archbishop of Mainz and the bishop of Brandenburg, in which he complained about Tetzel's indulgence-sales and the damage Tetzel's methods inflicted upon the faith of the common people. He also urged them, and particularly Albrecht of Mainz, to issue better instructions on the meaning of indulgences. In each case, Luther included a handwritten copy of 95 theses on the power of indulgences which he planned to propose for an academic disputation.

He proceeded in a correct way: he conformed to regular procedures and recognized the authority of his superiors. The archbishop of Mainz sent him no direct reply. He transmitted Luther's letter to his councillors, asked the theological faculty of Mainz for an opinion, and denounced Luther at the papal curia. The other bishops refused to take a position and limited themselves to warning Luther that he should not undertake anything in opposition to the papacy. In the meantime, Luther had sent his theses, apparently still in handwritten form, to some of his friends and correspondents, asking them for their reaction. Thus they came into circulation and were finally printed, but not on his initiative. They spread quickly and the whole cause became widely known, arousing growing excitement.

Luther then regarded himself as a loyal son of the church. His early writings show that he dreaded heresy and detested disobedience. By temperament and upbringing he was everything else but a revolutionary. But he was filled with a sense of mission. He attributed great importance to the fact that he was a doctor of theology and a professor of Biblical studies. He believed himself to have the authority to speak up in the name of Christ, the Word of God, against all that was wrong in the church and in Christendom. As his early lecture-notes on the Psalms and the Epistle to the Romans show, he was a man of a prophetic spirit. Thus he considered it his duty to criticize the schoolmen for their dependence upon Aristotelianism and to object to the arbitrariness of ecclesiastical and secular princes and their abuse of power. Indeed, while still at the beginning of his professorial career, he assumed responsibility for the introduction of radical changes in the theological curriculum at the University of Wittenberg: courses in Biblical theology replaced the traditional commentaries on Peter Lombard's Book of Sentences. What motivated him in this is well expressed in the outburst which is contained in his exposition of the eighth chapter of the Letter to the Romans, an outburst which he put down on paper but which (to judge from the students' note-books that have come down to us) he did not repeat in the classroom:

> "Indeed," he wrote, "I believe that I owe to the Lord this duty of crying out against philosophy and turning men to Holy Scripture. For, perhaps, if someone else who had been through it all were to do it, he would either be scared to do it or none would believe him. But I have been in the grind of these studies for lo, these many years and am worn out by it, and, on the basis of long experience, I have come to be persuaded that it is a vain study doomed to perdition. For this reason, I admonish you all as earnestly as I can: Be quickly done with these studies and let it be your only concern not to establish and to defend them but rather to deal with them as with bad skills that we learn only in order to get rid of them or with errors that we take up in order to refute them. . . . It is high time that we turn away from irrelevant studies and learn from Christ 'and him crucified'."[7]

It seems to me to have been Luther's distinctive nature that he was at the same time conservative and radical, a conserver as well as a reformer. He displayed this nature in all stages and phases of his life. For this reason, he broke with the priestly-sacramental traditions of the Roman Church and abolished monasticism, thus inaugurating a really new epoch in the history of Christianity. Yet he was no innovator and no revolutionary, and he never regarded himself as such. The reform which he advocated and which was ultimately carried through in the several Protestant churches was based, as he saw it and as also his followers and spiritual descendants came to see it, on the re-affirmation of the truth of the Christian gospel as he believed it had at all times been accessible to men in the Bible and in its picture of Christ. Adolf von Harnack wrote in his *History of Dogma*:

> Only in one respect was Luther great and powerful, enrapturing and irresistible, the lord of his epoch, striding victoriously over the history of a millennium, dislodging his own era and forcing it into a new course— he was great only in the re-discovery of the knowledge of God through the gospel, i.e., through Christ.[8]

Harnack found it necessary to couple this judgment with the following:

> It is a very one-sided, even perilous abstract consideration of Luther which sees in him the man of a new era, the hero of rising generations, or the creator of the modern spirit. Whosoever wishes to envisage such heroes must turn to Erasmus and his friends or to men like Denck, Franck, Servetus, and Bruno. In the periphery of his existence and also deep down in his being, Luther was an old-catholic, medieval phenomenon.[9]

Ernst Troeltsch was of the same opinion, and I too believe it must be sustained.

One can argue that, in his own way, Luther supports this view. In his "Smalcaldic Articles" of 1538 and particularly in his tract of 1541 entitled "Wider Hans Worst" he presents his own evaluation of his teachings and labors in their relation to the Roman Church and the history of Christianity.

In this latter writing, he tries to show in detail that he and his followers represent the true church, i.e., the Catholic Church as it prevailed in ancient times. He says there:

> The papists assert that they have remained in the old church as it existed since apostolic times. Hence they think that they are true heirs of the ancient church who have remained in it until now, but that we have fallen away from them and that we have formed a *new* church against them. To this I reply: What will you say if I show you that it is we who have stayed with the true ancient church, indeed that we are the true old church and that you, the papists, have broken with the ancient church and established a new church?[10]

Then he attempts to prove this by showing that he and the ancient church agree and have in common: 1. baptism, 2. the sacrament of the altar, 3. the keys, 4. the office of preaching God's word "without any addition, so he stresses, of any new human teaching."[11] Then he goes on to claim unity with the ancient church with respect to the use 5. of the Apostle's Creed, and 6. of the Lord's Prayer. The seventh and eighth points of agreement are the teachings on the power of the secular government and on marriage.

He then attempts to show that Roman Catholicism represents an

innovation through a defiance of the ancient church by the introduction of a religion requiring satisfactions and good works together
with the use of indulgences, pilgrimages and brotherhoods, the
transformation of the mass into a priestly sacrifice and of penance
into an exercise of priestly power. Finally he points to the papacy,
priestly celibacy and monasticism, the use of secular power by the
church, and the adoration of saints as deviations from the true church
as it prevailed in apostolic and post-apostolic times. Then he concludes:

> I am willing to recognize that the [Roman Catholic] Church is as much in
> continuity with the ancient church as we are and that it has the same
> baptism as we have and the sacrament and the keys and the text of the
> Bible and of the gospel. And I even go further than this and grant that we
> have received everything we have from the church among you (but not
> from you). What more do you want? Aren't we good enough for you?
> Can't you cease to regard us as heretics? We do not regard you as if you
> were Turks or Jews who are outside the church, but we say that you have
> not remained in the church [*yr bleibt nicht dabei*] and so you become the
> erring and disobedient church . . . which does not stay with the church in
> which it was born and raised. . . . Can't you understand this?[12]

In this sense Luther believed that he and the church for which he
spoke represented true Catholicism and that the Roman Church
which had declared him a heretic was sectarian.

What then shall we say by way of a conclusion about the "Catholic" Luther?

1. Because of his rediscovery of the gospel in the Bible and the
significance he attached to it—namely in so far as he was led to teach
that in the church as *communio sanctorum sive fidelium* a man is saved
by grace alone and faith alone on the basis and by the authority of
the Scripture alone and that he will manifest this salvation in and
through works of love in the natural ordinary pursuits of life—
Luther transcended Catholicism as understood by medieval theology
even before 1517 and ever after.

2. Luther did not hold the opinion that he had founded a new
church. For him the Reformation was a renewal of the ancient
Catholic Church.

3. He believed that this Catholicism was best expressed in the ancient Trinitarian and Christological dogmas and creeds.

4. These dogmas were Catholic, so he was persuaded, because he regarded them as true interpretations of Holy Scripture.

5. He believed that the Roman Church of his day had seceded from the Bible and the faith of the ancient church and was therefore sectarian.

6. He failed to see the historical continuity between the Bible, the ancient church, and Roman Catholicism.

7. He could rely on Biblical authority in the way in which he understood it and derive from it his profoundly Christian "pure doctrine" only because he practiced a Christological exegesis which was still unhistorical.

8. The Protestant principle of Scriptural authority, if historically understood and applied, implies necessarily the dissolution of the principle of Catholicism, if this means a unity or universality of a uniformitarian character.

9. Hence it is not very useful or helpful to speak of the "Catholic" Luther.

10. One should rather be concerned with the question: What contribution has Luther the "evangelist" (as he called himself) made and is he still able to make to a Christendom which in its modern setting is unavoidably pluralistic?[13]

NOTES

1. Joseph Lortz, "Martin Luther, Grundzüge seiner geistigen Struktur," in *Reformata reformanda, Festschrift für H. Jedin* (Münster, 1965), I, 216.

2. *Ibid.*, p. 217.

3. Joseph Lortz, *Die Reformation in Deutschland* (Freiburg, 1939–40), I, 120.

4. *Ibid.*, p. 162.

5. *Ibid.*, p. 402.

6. *Ibid.*, p. 394.

7. M. Luther, *Lectures on Romans* (Philadelphia, 1960), XV, 236.

8. A. v. Harnack, *Dogmengeschichte* (Tübingen, 1909), III, 812.

9. *Ibid.*, p. 809.

10. O. Clemen, *Luthers Werke in Auswahl* (Bonn, 1913), IV, 330.

11. *Ibid.*, p. 331. "We invent nothing new but keep and stay with the old Word of God as the ancient church had it. Hence together with the true ancient

church we are the one church which teaches and believes the one word of God. Hence the papists slander Christ, the apostles, and all Christendom when they call us innovators and heretics."

12. *Ibid.*, p. 340.

13. Cf. Walter von Loewenich, "Das Problem des katholischen Luther" in *Von Augustin zu Luther* (Witten, 1959), pp. 238–49.

4

The Essential Luther

JOHN T. McDONOUGH

FROM THE OUTSET I would like to state that a phenomenon as wide-spread and as powerful as the Reformation cannot be attributed to sin and error alone. The Reformation transformed the structures of the world, and thereby the very conditions in which millions of men had to work out their salvation. Could such a phenomenon occur without being part of God's design, without contributing something positive to our salvation? After all, God is Master of History, at least for the Christian.

One beneficial effect is now acknowledged by Catholic scholars: Luther forced the Church to take hold of herself and to reform herself, an action which is still going on today. And in this respect, it is true to say that Luther is partly responsible for saving the Church.

Moreover, because of him the Council of Trent undertook the great task of clearing the air, of dispelling the theological confusion of the sixteenth century. The conciliar Fathers formulated Catholic doctrine according to Holy Scripture. They avoided the language of the schools; they maintained a strict independence with respect to any scholastic conceptualization. Even today, the decrees of Trent can serve as a basis for fruitful dialogue between Catholics and Protestants. We owe this to Luther.

For this reason there is a growing consensus among Catholic scholars that Martin Luther, on the fundamental issue of the Reformation, was absolutely right. This issue was not politics, or economics, or indulgences, or papal authority, or even protest. It was simply the sovereignty of God. On this basic issue, Luther, in volumes of writings and thousands of sermons, preached to his contemporaries an entirely orthodox and truly Catholic doctrine: namely, that God alone—Father, Son and Holy Spirit—creates, redeems and sanctifies man.

If he differs from other Christian leaders on this issue, it is not so much in doctrinal innovation as in style and emphasis. And it is precisely here where I find the essential Luther—Luther the Reformer.

Everything he writes, preaches, experiences, is marked by and permeated with a vital awareness of the strength, the might, the overwhelming power of God's Word to make, remake and perfect man. And this I say, despite what we know to be his errors, his failings, his violence and rages and hatreds. He is so preoccupied—indeed so overcome—by the problem of man's salvation that he reads the Bible in a new way: as though the totality of his experience and the totality of his life were caused directly by his personal contact with the Word of God.

When studying Luther we should focus our eyes on this aspect of his person—that is, upon Luther as preacher of the Word. For, if we allow ourselves to be distracted by other aspects of his life and thought, we may be confused by the complexity of his personality and the massiveness of his statements, and even tempted to disparage the enduring value of his basic convictions.

Undeniably Luther is complex; in a sense he is more than a *homo duplex*; he is a *homo multiplex*: many persons in one man, so to speak. And this fact helps to explain the apparent lack of unity and system in his thought. There is Luther the young Catholic friar, Luther the early reformer, and Luther the mature resolute reformer. There is also Luther the polemicist, the doctor and professor, the poet and musician, and finally Luther the simple man of flesh and blood and human frailty. At times all of these "Luthers" seem at loggerheads, warring with one another. Yet, out of this complex man, growing in and through combat with himself, with the witnesses of traditional theology, with his adversaries, with the Roman Curia, emerges a religious genius—a *homo religiosus*.

Now it is my contention that by approaching Luther in this light— as a preacher of the Word, as a *homo religiosus*, singularly inspired and possessed by the power of God's saving Word—we can detect a certain unity in this man and in his writings.

When I say here, "a certain unity," I am not thinking of a unifying principle such as the notion of being in St. Thomas or the concept of predestination in Calvin; nor again of a preconceived plan which we project into his writings, in order to break down his theology into a system. Rather I am thinking of a central theme, a *Leitmotiv*, which emerges from both his experience and his writings, and which, in fact, underlies and determines his basic convictions. In other words a central theme which constitutes the very heart and core of the various parts of his teaching on the Bible, on faith, sin, grace, justification, redemption, sanctification, the Church, the Sacraments, prayer and good works. In short, I am thinking of his Law–Gospel doctrine of justification, entailing a despair–faith pattern of experience

What I mean here by his Law–Gospel doctrine, entailing a despair–faith pattern of experience, I described in my book as follows:

> The Word of God, which Luther defends and believes in, is two-fold: Decalogue precepts and promises and Gospel precepts and promises; or simply, the Word as Law and the Word as grace. Together they produce in sinful man an experience similar to Luther's own experience, namely a dynamic dualistic struggle of self-righteousness against God's righteousness which, in so far as God moves and graces man, terminates in a personal experience of despairing utterly in self and believing absolutely in Christ.[2]

The meaning of this doctrine is to make large the reality of God and make small the reality of man without God.

I have concluded, after careful study of Luther's writings, that this Law–Gospel doctrine is truly central to his basic convictions. It is precisely here that we find Luther one with himself, stubbornly consistent, resolute, unbending. His Law–Gospel doctrine becomes his profession of faith, his battle cry as a reformer.

When Luther opposes the shameful traffic in indulgences and the abuses of the sixteenth-century Church, with the Bible in his hands, he intends to preach his Law–Gospel "metanoia": God's Word as commandment and promise, causes in us a life-long despair–faith experience of penance.

Thus, in his treatise dedicated to Pope Leo X, entitled *The Liberty of the Christian Man*, he writes:

> When indeed, by the commandments, man has been shown his own impotence . . . then he is altogether humiliated and reduced to nothing in his own eyes and finds in himself nothing by which to be justified or saved. Here the other part of Scripture intervenes, the promises of God, and says: "If you wish to fulfil the Law, not to covet, as the law requires, then this is for you: believe in Christ in whom you are promised grace, peace, liberty and all things. . . ."[3]

Once we grasp Luther's intention and recognize his Law–Gospel manner of preaching the "metanoia," we begin to understand why he becomes the avowed enemy of scholasticism. If he rejects the language of the schoolmen and the language of Aristotle—the language of philosophy, logic and ethics—it is not because this language is unfamiliar or incomprehensible to him; on the contrary: it is because he prefers the prophetic, existential language of the Bible. He is not seeking to possess a speculative, theoretical knowledge of God, of grace, of sin, of Sacrament, but rather to be possessed by the living actual truth and power of God's Word. And in this sense he is, in resolve and purpose, a Christian preacher, a Christian reformer.

In matters of faith, he prefers to lay down and affirm his innermost convictions on the foundation of scripture and experience—irrespective of human authorities, logical necessities, and philosophical principles. Thus, we find him saying to Erasmus, at the end of his treatise *De servo arbitrio*, after setting out an array of scriptural arguments in favour of his thesis: "I have not wanted to compare or to confront but to affirm, and I affirm."[4]

And in affirming, he insists on his role as a doctor of the Church; he insists that his doctrine is a pure doctrine—pure in the sense that it is based, in his deepest conviction, purely and simply on the Word of God—and he teaches it as decisive and binding on man's conscience. In this respect, he is not subjective.

For him the fundamental message of the Gospel is objectively apparent to any man who reads the scriptures with an honest mind and open heart. And that message is simply this: Christ is our Lord and Saviour, crucified and resurrected for our sins. This message, he further claims, is so manifest and obvious in the language of the scriptures that we need no pope, bishop, or priest to interpret its basic meaning for us.

Catholic scholars, in the past, have failed to perceive this essential Luther because they were, in my opinion, prisoners of Greek philosophy and scholastic theology. Instead of interpreting Luther in his own context—the dynamic experiential context of the prophet and the preacher—they attempted to reduce his strong sinewy metaphors and wild paradoxes to logical categories. In this way it was easy for them to point to contradictions and absurdities in his teachings.

Thus we find men like Denifle, Grisar, Maritain, even Bouyer and others, misunderstanding Luther's statements about man's enduring sinfulness or the Christian's passive and imputed righteousness. I, myself, in my own book on Luther, did likewise. Only now in the age of ecumenism am I beginning to see the light.

If we think of Luther's assertion, "man is essentially corrupt," as referring to a *mutatio simpliciter*, in the Aristotelian sense, then logically Luther is more than a pessimist—he is a nihilist. But Luther knew that man, the sinner, remains essentially man. Sin does not cause him to change substantially or essentially. But this is not what Luther, the preacher, means at all. He is simply telling us that before God—*coram Deo*—man is always conscious of being a sinner. And this feeling or consciousness obtains after Baptism as well as before. If he insists on our corruption, in lurid and even unreasonable terms, it is because he wishes to make us aware of the reality of sin, the reality of our ungodly selfishness.

Again, if we wish to argue with Luther over his notion of passive righteousness, as Erasmus did, accusing him of denying all freedom to man, we fall into the same logical trap. We fail to understand Luther's basic intention. Luther was no fool. He knew very well that man is free. When he speaks of "justitia passiva," he simply means to say that man cannot command God to give us faith and grace and forgiveness. In this context, man can only wait, as the Jews wait, and receive His gifts. Luther therefore preaches that we must experience despair about our own merits in order to experience faith in Christ's infinite merits. I personally think that is all he really means by "justitia passiva."

And this helps us understand his notion of imputed righteousness —"justitia reputata." Theologians, Protestant and Catholic alike, have been "hung up" too long on this question. The Protestants develop contrived arguments from Scripture by way of justifying Luther's notion; and the Catholics see the notion as a denial of the efficacy of God's Word and sacraments to redeem and sanctify us ontologically. But what again does Luther, as preacher and prophet, really mean here? I say he means this: he wishes us to understand that no matter what God does to us or for us, in the order of creation and grace, we are ever conscious of an infinite gap or abyss between ourselves and the Godhead. To feel certitude that, somehow, the gap has been bridged by Christ, we must think of our righteousness in some respect as imputed, not absolutely acquired or possessed.

The effort today to trace Luther's notion of imputed righteousness to nominalism is interesting and, indeed, meaningful from an historical point of view. Is it really relevant to the basic issue of the Reformation? I am not sure, though in my own book I did imply that it was. Louis Bouyer in his work, *Du protestantisme à l'église*, is right to point out the influence of nominalism on Luther. And the "voluntarism" of Luther's theology certainly smacks of Gabriel Biel. But is this evidence enough to conclude that Lutheranism is the product of nominalism?

Again I say that if we study Luther in his proper context—that of the evangelical preacher seeking to convert men to God— there is certainly a sense in which we can speak of our faith, hope and charity as an imputed righteousness. We are always aware, in our faith, that, without God's mercy and love, we are nothing; unless He accepts us as we are, we are damned. Is that fact not the fundamental basis of imputed righteousness? Is that not precisely what Luther is saying?

It is essentially, fundamentally Luther's Law-Gospel doctrine which inaugurates the immense and tragic debate which we call the

"Reformation." For Luther this doctrine of justification preaches the most important, the most demanding, of Christian teaching: namely, the "metanoia" of the Bible. His Law-Gospel preaching places all the emphasis on man's spiritual poverty. "Man suffers deeply from his desire to relate everything to himself, from what Luther calls man's *incurvitas*. Yet, in reality, man without God is nothing, and this he must recognize."[5] That is why Luther cries out furiously, violently, against the spiritual worth of man's efforts without God. He wants men, in the realm of the spirit, to hope only in the righteousness of Christ.

To my mind, this is the significance of Luther's battle cry—*sola scriptura, sola gratia, sola fide*—and the reason why he was willing to risk everything for it: his mind, his soul, and at the Diet of Worms in 1521 even his head.

If he is impulsive, obstinate, rash, if subjective in his preaching and experience, failing to grasp the total content of the scriptures and the teachings of the Church, it is not because he is intentionally egocentric, selfish or biased; rather it is because this Law-Gospel "metanoia" is for him all and everything, exclusively, completely, and solely. He relates everything to his experience and understanding of the Law and the Gospel.

And herein lies the grandeur and the tragedy of Luther: sometimes magnificently, at all times passionately, in deep and sincere faith, he defended the "metanoia" of the Bible. But, through an excessive one-sidedness, necessary for his times, he became unintentionally instrumental in establishing a church within the Church, called Lutheran. He himself would consider this a tragedy, for he did not want his Church to be called by any other name than that of Christ.

None the less it is because of Luther, and because of Protestantism today, that we are aware that all is not right with Holy Mother the Church. Many areas of her jurisdiction and teachings, which Luther criticized and attacked, must undergo a sharp and searching scrutiny in the light of the new Biblical studies, the new theology, and twenty centuries of Church history.

Luther did not break with Rome because he was lacking in faith or because he had abandoned Christ. On the contrary, his whole life was one of enduring faith, and all his preaching Christ-centred. As he declared in his *Commentary on the Epistle to the Galatians*: "For that one doctrine which I have supremely at heart is that of faith in Christ, in whom, through whom, and unto whom all my theological thinking flows back and forth day and night."

Thus the Church must subordinate everything in her life to this one truth, this one reality, this one event: Christ. Everything must be secondary and subordinated to Christ. To accept Luther's challenge Catholics and Protestants must show that their liturgical life, their private devotions, their obedience to authority, their loyalty to popes and bishops, their theology and their daily lives are nothing more or less than the extension of Christ in time and space for the salvation of the world.

And what does this mean in practice? It means this: the Church is not the extension of Greek philosophy, or fourth-century Latin, or Roman Law, or medieval scholasticism, or Renaissance politics, or nineteenth-century obscurantism, or twentieth-century pessimism. It is simply the extension of the crucified and resurrected Christ. Thus everything which aids and promotes this extension is sacred before God—indeed, grace; everything that hinders or obstructs this extension is profane—in Luther's language, man-made works. Until the Church makes this point perfectly clear to the whole world, Martin Luther's challenge still stands.

NOTES

1. Joseph Lortz, "Martin Luther," in *Découverte de l'oecuménisme* (Paris, 1961), p. 350.
2. *The Law and the Gospel in Luther* (Oxford, 1963), p. 1. See this work for a more detailed analysis of this doctrine and experience.
3. *D. Martini Luthers Werke* (Weimar, 1883—), VII, 52–55.
4. *Ibid.*, XVIII, 787.
5. Lortz, *op. cit.*

5

Luther and the Princes

HAJO HOLBORN

THE RAPID SPREAD of Luther's ideas after 1517 remains one of the most miraculous events in history. What began as a controversy among scholars produced before long an echo all over Germany and beyond, and amazingly enough from all classes of society. This reaction showed that all classes in Germany held grievances and desired a reform of society. Luther's creed appeared to many a more satisfying faith than scholasticism had offered. Moreover Luther's fight against hierarchy and the papacy seemed to open the road for political and social reform as well. Luther's ideas stirred up the various social groups, but at the same time strengthened the antagonism between them. The knights' rebellion of 1522 did not find the support of the common man or of the cities, and the secular princes easily defeated the turbulent knights. The great peasants' revolution of 1525 was opposed by the cities, as well as by the nobility, and in the end was put down by the secular princes. After 1525 the princes were unquestionably the strongest political force in Germany, and logically the survival of German Protestantism rested in their hands. For the dissemination of Luther's ideas the German cities were of the greatest importance. By 1560 all the imperial free cities, with the exception of Cologne, Aachen, and some small places in Alsace and the southwest of the Empire, had adopted Protestantism.[1] But the cities conducted very cautious policies. After 1530 the commerce of the German cities declined and also their political influence, which never had been dominant, waned. The fate of German Protestantism was decided by the princes. Although the German cities made great contributions to the religious life of Protestantism, the churches in

67

the various principalities became the more typical form of German Protestantism.[2]

The German principalities or territorial states around 1500 were no absolutist states. Their government was divided between the princes and the estates. Sometimes the two forces paralyzed each other, but more often the princes gained an edge on the estates. Naturally the princes endeavored to win independent power. But inevitably they had to frame their policies, particularly with regard to the church, with an eye to the estates. For a long time ecclesiastical matters had been the concern of the princely governments. The great schism had compelled the princes to assume greater control of the church in their territories. After the councils of Constance and Basel, however, the restored papacy reasserted its authority. In Germany, with its innumerable princes and lands, the claims of the papacy could be more fully realized than in the national monarchies of Spain, France, and England.

The chief complaints against Rome were about the money that the Vatican extracted from the German Empire either in the form of taxes or spoils. In addition the ecclesiastical courts had a far-reaching jurisdiction that might affect the life of every individual. Not only were all clerics exempted from the princely courts but also laymen could be brought before an ecclesiastical court and, in cases where an appeal was taken, this meant the courts of Rome. This interference was particularly resented in Germany, and in this matter there was no difference of opinion among the princes and their estates since both wanted their territories self-contained and not open to intrusion in their internal life. The struggle over the jurisdiction of the ecclesiastical courts had been going on for a century before Luther appeared. And at least in the more powerful principalities some progress had been achieved—particularly in the Habsburg territories, but also in the Electorate of Saxony and the Duchy of Jülich-Cleve. In many places the princes had acquired a considerable part of the church government.

The position of the princes was based chiefly on their role as patrons and advocates of the church. Many church buildings, monasteries, or benefices had been the gift of the ruling dynasty.

In addition, the princes inherited patrons' rights from noble families which died out. Their rights as advocates (*Vögte*) stemmed from the rule that only arms-bearers could appear before the secular courts. As patrons and advocates of the churches and monasteries in their lands, the princes endeavored to gain greater control over the indigenous church. The practice was very different from what was still the official theory. The medieval theory of government assumed that it was the function of the secular arm to realize justice. But since only the church could define justice, the secular branch had to recognize the superiority of the church. The secular branch had as its main function the protection of the church and for that reason had to grant the clergy two powers, the *potestas ordinis* and the *potestas jurisdictionis*. The *potestas ordinis* was the clerical power to distribute through sacred objects and formulas the supernatural force of divine grace which the individual members of the church needed for their salvation. The *potestas jurisdictionis* was the right of the church to order and execute what was necessary to keep the members of the church on the right path. Luther abolished the *potestas ordinis* altogether and left little of the *potestas jurisdictionis*. To him the church was endowed only with the word of God. And the power of the church was confined to the sermon, the administration of sacraments, and the spiritual care of the individual church members. The hierarchy, including the papacy, appeared to Luther as a sinful abomination.

Thereby the position of the church in the world was totally changed.[3] In the full sense Luther saw the church and Christianty only in the invisible, though real, community of redeemed Christians. But he retained the conception of Christianity as a civil community of Christian peoples. Usually he avoids the term "church" for the church visible and prefers to talk merely about *Gemeinde* (congregation). It needs an outward organization which, however, may vary according to time and circumstances.

Luther had originally advised the new believers to withdraw from priests as well as to give up the mass and other objectionable rituals. Instead they should come together in order to serve the Gospel. If necessary they should assemble at homes and should elect certain members to preach the word, administer baptism and the Lord's supper, bless marriages, and do everything that a congregation needed. If, however, a whole congregation was won by the new doctrine, it should have the right to arrange its ecclesiastical organization in every respect according to the Gospel. With regard to these congregations Luther thought for a while of organizing them on two levels: one that would bring together the nominal Christians for whom a richer ritual would be designed and among whom the minister should perform his religious and educational work, and, as the second, the much closer circle of the earnest and true Christians who would worship for their common edification only through Word and sacrament in their simplest forms. The two levels would be held together by the ministerial office, whose task it would be to lead people from the wider circle into the select group. But Luther finally rejected such an organization. Since it was God's will that His Word should reach everybody, the true Christians out of Christian love had to remain with all the people in the same congregation.

In the years 1522–25 Luther had wished to reform the church through the parishes. He had freed the secular governments from subordination to ecclesiastical authorities. But he maintained the medieval idea that the secular governments had an important function with regard to the church. To be true, the secular governments were excluded from any influence on the invisible church, which is dominated only by the Word and motivated by freedom and love. In contrast, the secular governments act through law and force. They must use these attributes to protect the pious, suppress crime and injustice, but also to advance the preaching of the Gospel and do away with the perversions of the papal system, particularly the mass.

Until 1525 Luther drew a distinction between the local authorities and the land authorities. The local rulers, either town councillors or noblemen, were to assume the leadership in the reforms, though together with the congregations. The land government was only to protect the parishes against external resistance and might admonish but not rule if the reform was lagging. But the parishes, particularly those in the villages that constituted the vast majority, proved incapable of reforming the church by their own efforts. Chaotic conditions developed. Ecclesiastical life ceased in some parishes, while others diverged in widely different directions. Moreover Anabaptism and Sectarianism appeared and endangered the Word of God. In this situation it seemed necessary to reconstruct the bishop's office in some fashion. In the emergency that existed, Luther found that the prince as the *praecipuum membrum ecclesiae* was to arrange for a visitation. He was to act, however, not in his capacity as a secular ruler but as a member of the church or Christian brother. Luther emphasized that the prince had no part in the church government and was not a Christian teacher. In appointing a visitation committee he only helped to make the visitation possible for which the church was waiting. The only two functions which in connection with the visitation Luther assigned to the prince seemed to him duties of secular government. The first was the administration of the church property; the second was an action for the maintenance of public peace: the removal from the princely territory of those who refused to accept the creed of the majority. To Luther these distinctions were clear.

But they did not carry great weight with the princes. When the elector of Saxony announced the visitation in 1527, he stated that he ordered it on the strength of his authority as territorial ruler. The visitors, both ministers and jurists, were his officials who in the elector's name would tell the parishes what their obligations were with regard both to the external order and to the faith. Nobody, the announcement said, should dare to teach, preach, or administer the sacraments otherwise than according to God's Word as it had been accepted by the prince. The elector, so it was said, did not want to enforce on anybody what he should believe; but since in order to avoid revolt he would not tolerate sects or separation in his lands, he commanded those who disagreed with him, ministers as well as laymen, to leave his lands. In this announcement the elector appears as responsible for the spiritual welfare of his subjects as much as for their physical welfare. The elector's instruction was actually the establishment of the government of the territorial ruler over the church in his land (*landesherrliches Kirchenregiment*).

Luther's dissent from this system proved of no avail. The system was readily accepted, partly because the trend towards a state church had already gone very far before the Reformation. Seldom did the princes, at least in the sixteenth century, declare their position vis-à-vis the church an inherent right of princely office. Mostly it was explained as the duty of the Christian prince to care not only for the physical but also for the spiritual welfare of his subjects. But the German princes might have claimed that the spiritual jurisdiction in their territories had come to them through the Treaty of Passau and the Religious Peace of Augsburg.

Luther always emphasized that the princes had no right to interfere in the administration of the Word and that they were bound by it as much as any Christian. But once controversies arose over what was evangelical truth, the secular governments had to decide what they wanted to recognize and consequently protect as truth, and what errors they wanted to suppress. Thus the secular government was able to subordinate the ministers to its will. The Lutheran churches according to Luther were chiefly institutes for spreading the pure doctrine. And this he made the mission of specially trained pastors. Therefore the congregations themselves remained excluded from the only truly ecclesiastical work. They were made exclusively the objects of pastoral labor, while the secular governments were responsible for the external conditions of the church and the protection against any doctrinal error.

If we now turn to the question of why princes became Protestants, we must at once state that there is no simple answer because there is no single cause. The most important figure among the German territorial princes was, of course, Luther's own prince. We know that Frederick the Wise himself cultivated some of the pious practices of the old religion. Thus he took great pride in the large collection of saintly relics which he had brought together in Wittenberg. On the other hand, as a ruler he had gone very far in subjecting the church of his electorate to his princely administration.[4] He was obviously impressed that the university, which he had founded, supported Luther from the outset. And in his entourage there were good many people who pleaded for Luther.

In general the role of the princely councillors can hardly be exaggerated for the history of the Reformation. Many of them were influenced by the ideas of humanistic reform and at the same time eager to build up the authority and power of their princes. Even those councillors and princes who felt that Luther's critique of the official religion went much too far, particularly his teachings on the sacraments, felt that Luther's attack on the abuses of the papacy and hierarchy could be employed for good political ends. When Luther disappointed any expectations that he might compromise on his religious doctrines by his stand at the Diet of Worms, these men could argue that, in view of Luther's popular support, the enforcement of the Edict of Worms was impossible unless the Roman Church first took drastic steps towards an internal reform. Therefore from the outset the spread of Lutheranism was a political problem of the first order.

There can be no doubt that a good many princes were moved to embrace Protestantism by personal religious conviction. Many others, however, particularly after 1530, became Protestants for political reasons. The seizure of church property proved one of the great temptations. Even in places where the princes had to divide the church property with the nobility they gained new resources for conducting more active policies. Moreover the position as *summus episcopus* and the assumption of responsibility for public education and social welfare gave the princely office more far-reaching tasks and a heightened dignity. In this respect the period of the Reformation meant a new stage in the evolution of absolute monarchy in Germany. It should not be forgotten, however, that a similar development can be observed on the Catholic side.

Till 1560 the Catholic Church in Germany proved so weak that it would not have survived if it had not possessed the protection of a number of powerful princes—beginning, of course, with Emperor Charles V and King Ferdinand. In Bohemia, Austria, Styria, and also in Bavaria, the nobility largely turned to Protestantism and made the religious issue the means for advancing its political power. The ultimate defeat of Protestantism in these territories in the Thirty Years' War meant at the same time the complete defeat of the estates and the establishment of absolutist government. The power of the state over the church was very great in the subsequent centuries even in Catholic countries. But the survival of the hierarchy and papacy made it possible for the church to recover an independent position in the nineteenth century.

The dominant role that the Protestant Reformation assigned to the princes did not lead by itself to the establishment of absolutist government, although it contributed to its development. But once absolutist governments came into existence in Protestant countries these governments further extended their rule over the church and the Protestant churches proved incapable of extricating themselves from the control of the state during the nineteenth century. The inner life of religion was thereby gravely impaired.

NOTES

1. Ernst W. Zeeden, *Die Entstehung der Konfessionen* (Munich-Vienna, 1965), p. 16.
2. A more extensive treatment of the political and religious development is contained in my *A History of Modern Germany*, Vol. I: *The Reformation* (New York: Knopf, 1959).
3. The best study of the development of Luther's conception of the church is still Karl Holl, "Die Enstehung von Luthers Kirchenbegriff" and "Luther und das landesherrliche Kirchenregiment" in his *Gesammelte Aufsätze zur Kirchengeschichte*, Vol. I: *Luther* (2nd ed. Tübingen, 1923), pp. 288–380.
4. See Paul Kirn, *Friedrich der Weise und die Kirche* (Leipzig, 1926).

6

The Reformation and the
Urban Social Classes
in Germany

HAROLD J. GRIMM

LATE IN MARCH, 1526, several years before the Hanseatic cities of
Lübeck and Lüneburg became Protestant, the burgomaster and
council of the former sent the burgomaster and council of the latter
a copy of a letter from a Lübeck merchant in London, calling atten
tion to the danger that faced persons who brought Lutheran books
to the Steelyard.[1] The letter from London points to the seriousness of
this situation by stating that "a certain knight, Thomas More," had
arrested eight persons in the Steelyard for having Lutheran books in
their possession.[2] This and many similar instances illustrate the fact
that merchants played an important part in spreading the Reformation to European commercial centers. Accordingly, one of the most
fruitful areas of study with respect to the rapid spread of the Reformation is the interest of the merchants and other urban classes in
Germany, especially in the free imperial cities. Although scholars
have analyzed various aspects of city life at the close of the Middle
Ages in great detail, they have done relatively little by way of
explaining why representatives of the different urban classes embraced the Reformation from its very beginnings. Since the movement is highly complicated, much detailed study of individual
townsmen, their city councils, and their religious and cultural back-
grounds is necessary before we can make more than cautious, tentative generalizations.

Because there were great differences among the German cities with respect to their political, constitutional, religious, social, and cultural developments, historians have found it advisable to begin a study of the reception of the Reformation by the various urban classes by examining the free imperial cities which had much in common. As Bernd Moeller has pointed out, there were eight-five cities listed as "frei- und reichstett' at the Diet of Worms in 1521 and sixty-five of these actually were directly under the authority of the emperor. Of this number, more than fifty officially recognized the Reformation in the sixteenth century and more than half of these accepted and retained Protestantism.[3]

An obvious explanation for the acceptance of a novel, revolutionary program lies in widespread dissatisfaction. Rulers in the imperial cities were compelled to take cognizance of the dissatisfaction among their people in their attempts to provide for the general welfare of their communities. Responsible for the unrest in the cities as well as everywhere in Germany at the beginning of the sixteenth century were: the development of territorial states which were infringing on the medieval, feudal rights of all other political entities, including the empire; the changing political character of the cities, largely a consequence of their struggles with the territorial princes; the introduction of Roman Law, which was rapidly replacing feudal, customary law; the commercial revolution, which resulted in important changes in methods of production and distribution as well as in avenues of trade; the emergence of capitalism with its increasing concentrations of wealth, concomitant spread of poverty, and eventual destruction of the medieval guild system; the secularization of the church in the face of a growing concern over religious matters; the spread of learning, which no longer remained a monopoly of the church; the rapidly expanding printing of books and pamphlets by means of which an increasingly literate population became actively concerned with the world about it and learned about novel programs of action.

To arrive at an understanding of why the dissatisfied social groups of the cities so readily accepted the Reformation, one must evaluate their positive heritage. This consisted of three important elements: first, the medieval ideals, attitudes, and experiences of the free members of urban communes who had worked out a *modus vivendi* among themselves and with their feudal lords; second, the practical, late-medieval mysticism with its emphasis on inner spirituality and ethics; third, humanism, which many educated townsmen embraced as a culture reflecting their urban interests and giving them a social status they had lacked during the height of feudal chivalry.

The society of the medieval German city was not divided into classes in the modern sense of the term. Luther and his contemporaries spoke of the various urban groups as "estates," each having its special interests and duties but all contributing to the *Gemeinwohl*, or general welfare of the community. To speak of a capitalist class or of a proletariat, for example, would lead to a complete misunderstanding of social conditions in late-medieval German cities. The citizens of the earliest communes were free persons who had banded together as *Eidgenossenschaften*, or *conjurationes*, to seek independence from their local feudal lords, often bishops. To retain their independence, the citizens and city councils of many communes instituted the annual oath, the *conjuratio reiterata*, which persisted into the sixteenth century. Furthermore, citizenship was obtained by swearing an oath to maintain the general welfare.[4]

Although "it is impossible to connect the Reformation world of thought with any particular social class," as Ernst Troeltsch has pointed out, there is "an indirect connection with bourgeois growth in the cities,"[5] and it will prove helpful to examine the interests of the various groups within the cities. In the typical imperial city, leadership soon fell into the hands of the patricians, usually wealthy landowners or merchants who devoted their time and talents, with little or no remuneration, to the welfare of their fellow citizens. It was natural that those who carried the chief burdens of government should constitute smaller councils within the original large ones and then perpetuate themselves and their families in office and social status. That the movement from ordinary citizenship to the patrician class was relatively easy, however, can be seen by the situation in Nuremberg, where in 1511 only thirty-seven *ehrbaren*, or honorable, families had been represented among the hundred and eighteen listed in 1390.[6] In Augsburg some of the new patricians came from the artisan class, including the Fuggers and Höchstetters. After 1500, however, when the medieval cities began to decline, the status of the patricians became much less flexible.

At the beginning of the Reformation, the authority of the patricians varied from place to place. In Nuremberg, Frankfurt a. M., Rostock, Stralsund, and Wismar, for example, they were in complete control of the councils, while in Augsburg, Ulm, Strasburg, Regensburg, Rothenburg o. T., and Schwäbisch Hall they shared their authority with representatives of the guilds, and in Speyer and Schlettstadt the guilds controlled the councils.[7] In nearly all the cities, however, the patricians retained considerable influence, for only they had the time and money to devote to municipal matters and to go on long diplomatic missions for the council.[8] The great majority of patricians were sincerely concerned with serving the general welfare in their cities.

There were patricians in virtually every large German city who accepted Lutheranism at an early date. While few of these did so for economic and social reasons, some did so in spite of them. Caspar Nützel, second in authority in the city council of Nuremberg, for example, had a German translation of Luther's ninety-five theses published for popular consumption. Jerome Ebner of the same council supported the Reformation from its beginnings. Lazarus Spengler, the council's *Ratsschreiber*, or syndic, played the leading role in the events which led to the introduction of the Reformation in Nuremberg in the spring of 1525.

The artisans, who comprised the great majority of the citizens of the free imperial cities, formed guilds as the best means for playing their respective roles in their communities and, in many instances, for obtaining a share in governing them. In most of the cities, they succeeded during the turbulent times of the latter half of the fourteenth century. The masters of the most important guilds who became councilors joined the ranks of the patricians and frequently spoke of themselves as *ehrbar*. Whether or not they shared in governing their cities, the artisans were proud of the parts they played in providing for the general welfare and identified themselves with their cities and the empire as members of their guilds. Their emphasis upon equality and brotherhood and their experiences in managing their own affairs help explain their dissatisfaction with the tendency of the patricians to acquire and retain exclusive authority.

The artisans generally were receptive to the doctrines of Luther and later especially of Zwingli and Bucer. The Reformation witnessed a considerable improvement of the economic and social status of the artisans and of the broad middle class as well as a democratization of administration and legal justice until territorial princes brought most of the cities under their control.[9] But to state that "the same class which supported the Reformation had as its political goal the democratization of the city government" is an erroneous generalization.[10] Cities in which artisans had obtained partial or complete control were as a rule as conservative as those dominated by the patricians.

Most dissatisfied with their status in the late medieval cities were the members of the small guilds who lived from hand to mouth and often were the objects of charity—such as the gardeners, vintners, and small farmers, all of whom once had made respectable livings; inhabitants of the suburbs who constituted a kind of second-class citizenry outside the walls; free laborers and mercenary foot soldiers who comprised a colorful floating population; journeymen who in increasing numbers found it impossible to become masters of guilds and who, because of their contacts with journeymen in other cities and their possession of at least the rudiments of education, frequently became leaders of these classes. Otherwise, these people had little in common except dissatisfaction with their economic and social status and distrust of those in power. At the beginning of the Reformation, about a half of the population of Augsburg and a fifth of the population of Hamburg, to use but two examples, were propertyless.[11] Although this was a highly volatile social group which readily joined Reformation leaders, especially those of the left-wing movements, it is wrong to conclude that they did so solely for economic reasons.

Common to all the social groups of the late-medieval imperial cities was, as we have seen, a sense of unity and a feeling of responsibility for the general welfare, an inheritance of the slogan of antiquity, *salus publica suprema lex*, revived in Carolingian times and incorporated in feudal institutions and laws as *communis utilitas*. The *Eidgenos-*

sen, or associates by oath, of the emerging cities, and the guilds, both merchant and craft, made the general welfare the chief objective of their oaths and corporate existence for without this they could not have existed. The individual was not the center of urban concern, nor was the family, nor even the guild, but the entire community.[12]

In the medieval city there was no distinction between the secular and the spiritual, the political community and the religious congregation, for it was a little *corpus Christianum* in which there were both secular and spiritual functions controlled by the community as a whole for the general welfare and performed by the city council which represented the community. There was no church-state dichotomy as in modern times. The attempts of the councils to bring the church into the communities go back into the high Middle Ages. The fact that the clergy, often foreigners or persons appointed by ecclesiastical authorities outside the city, resisted this tendency led to a feeling of hostility toward them. They did not accept the responsibilities of citizens such as paying taxes, building defenses, and manning walls. On the other hand, they had all the advantages of citizens, often engaged in what was considered unfair economic competition with the merchants, accumulated property which became tax-free, and were subject to trial only by their own canon-law courts.[13] It is no wonder that citizens became particularly critical when the secularization of the church in the late Middle Ages was accompanied by neglect of spiritual functions and corruption.

In the fifteenth century, long before the Reformation, numerous city councils began to insist upon reforms in monasteries, control over the selection of abbots and priors, the administration of church properties and endowments, the supervision of hospitals, assistance in the selection of the secular clergy and the provosts of parish churches, care of the poor, and regulation of education. By the time of the Reformation, there was ample precedent for assumption of ecclesiastical functions by the city councils. When the bishop of Bamberg demanded that the city council of Nuremberg hand over the two Protestant provosts of the two parish churches for trial in his court, the council refused to do so and wrote the bishop a lengthy letter in which it argued much of its case on the basis of precedent.[14]

There were few communities in which the citizens did not agree with their city councils that the medieval concern for the general welfare should become also a concern for the general salvation.

The pride of the citizens of the free imperial cities in their communities and their firm conviction in their right to control all their affairs for the general welfare stemmed to a large degree from their conception of their cities as imperial in a real sense. As the Holy Roman Empire of the German Nation began to decline in the thirteenth century, the cities rose in power and influence, and assumed that they were the empire, a significant part of the entire *corpus Christianum*, who had received their rights and freedoms from their kings and emperors. The presence of the imperial regalia in Nuremberg, for example, strengthened the feeling of her citizens that their city and the empire and Christendom were one.[15] This explains to a large degree the attitude of her city council toward Emperor Charles V after the formal adoption of Lutheranism in 1525. Nuremberg consistently remained loyal to him.

Despite the strong sense of unity in the imperial cities, there were numerous threats to this heritage which help explain the widespread dissatisfaction on the eve of the Reformation. Most important was the development of territorial states which compelled the German cities themselves to take on the characteristics of the territorial state to survive.[16] Some of them, like Nuremberg, accumulated territories, began to participate as regular estates in the imperial diets, enlarged and strengthened their city councils, and eventually developed bureaucratic administrations with salaried officials, all of which led to a weakening of the sense of the general welfare and of the unity of secular and religious functions in one *corpus Christianum*.

The rapid spread of the Reformation to the free imperial cities can be explained also by the fact that all the urban classes were greatly concerned about religious matters at the close of the Middle Ages, especially about such theological problems as worried the young Luther and about ethical questions arising out of fundamental economic, political, and social changes.[17] When earnest preachers of such monastic orders as the Dominicans, Franciscans, and Augustinian Eremites touched on these problems in forceful kerygmatic sermons, large audiences came to hear them. Lazarus Spengler, for example, took copious notes on the sermons of John von Staupitz, prior-general of the Augustinians, when he preached in Nuremberg. So strong was the influence of Staupitz there that the circle of intellectual élite which had devoted its discussions to humanist interests came to be called the *Sodalitas Staupitziana.* The inner spirituality, direct simplicity, and ethical earnestness of those who had been influenced by Christian mysticism appealed especially to the educated laymen of the imperial cities. In the spread of the Reformation these laymen usually played more active roles than the clergy.

Christian humanism also furthered the cause of the Reformation, especially among the intellectual élite in southern Germany.[18] Christian humanists generally evinced a strong interest in the Bible, in the writings of the church Fathers, and in a renewed emphasis on ethical standards, both classical and Christian, as applied to both secular and spiritual institutions. The Nuremberg circle of intelligentsia, which included several councilmen, corresponded on religious subjects with many people, including the humanist Pirckheimer's sister Caritas, abbess of the Franciscan convent of St. Clara in Nuremberg; made use of the council library which contained books on science, theology, and the classics; read works of the church Fathers, particularly of St. Jerome, whom Albrecht Dürer portrayed ten times in his art and a short biography of whom Spengler published; became much interested in the sermons of the well-educated Augustinians—John von Staupitz, Wenzel Linck, and Martin Luther.

Lazarus Spengler illustrated his concern for a practical, mystical piety and Christian humanist ethics by publishing in 1520 his *Admonition and Instruction for a Virtuous Life,* dedicated to his friend Albrecht Dürer. In it he listed as outstanding virtues the fear of God, acceptance of suffering, reasonableness, friendship, loyalty, modesty, humility, discretion, restraint, trustworthiness, compassion, and love of peace—evidences of Stoic, humanist, and burgher influences. Although these interests by no means led directly to the Reformation, they helped make many persons receptive to Reformation theology.

The first generation of Protestant reformers enunciated a theology, the social implications of which appealed to the urban classes, particularly those who were dissatisfied with religious conditions in their communities.[19] Luther's revolutionary doctrine of the universal priesthood of believers, for example, emphasized the responsibility of the individual to God in opposition to the sharp medieval distinction between the laity and the clergy, thereby justifying the basis for the idea of the *Genossenschaft* by stressing the equality of all citizens before God.[20] By ennobling every calling of man as a divine service, he also underscored the obligation of every Christian to serve the general welfare.[21] On the other hand, his stressing of the individual rather than the community helped destroy the medieval conception of the *corpus Christianum* with its identification of the city corporation and the religious congregation.

Ulrich Zwingli strongly identified the two functions in the medieval city by erecting a theocracy in Zurich and demanding that Christians create a new Zion here on earth. For him the visible and the invisible church became one. The visible church was duty bound to interpret the Bible as a law for the city through its leaders as the prophets had done in the Old Testament, while the city council was expected to assure the correct preaching of the Gospel.

Martin Bucer, whose *De regno Christi* had a big influence not only on German townsmen but on Calvinism and Anglicanism, also furthered the medieval conception that the city corporation and its church congregation were one and that both led men to Christ, with love as the guiding principle.[22] The Holy Spirit, he maintained, lives in the church as the communion of the elect, as a visible church, while the government on the basis of a community ethics must serve the secular and spiritual needs of its citizens by providing pastors and teachers, educating children, and exiling heretics. Matters of faith and theology, however, were to be reserved for the clergy.

Apparently the leaders of the Reformation in the cities were not aware of the political implications of the theology of the reformers and little can be adduced to prove that they were immediately influenced by them. The most that can be stated at the present time is that the views of Zwingli and Bucer were preferred by most of the cities in southern Germany and that the merchants and artisans there seem to have favoured the greater simplicity of Zwingli's church service, his opposition to images in houses of worship, and his interpretation of the Lord's Supper.

The urban classes of Germany, particularly of the free imperial cities, were, as a whole, sincerely religious at the beginning of the sixteenth century and took the Reformation seriously. They were dissatisfied by the church's inability to provide religious satisfaction and were prepared to discuss and act upon the issues raised by the movement because of their urban traditions and experiences, education, preaching, and the reading of books and pamphlets. Some members of the ruling families, especially in southern Germany, were further prepared for the reception of the Reformation by the spread of Christian mysticism and Christian humanism.

The Reformation in Germany was essentially a folk movement, touching all segments of society. In most instances the city councils, conservative as they were, eventually gave way to the demands of their citizens and called evangelical preachers who gradually carried out the requested changes in form and doctrine. Accordingly, the reception of the Reformation by the urban classes was in harmony with medieval urban ideals and practices; yet it produced revolutionary results. Many city councils, as representatives of their respective communities, acted for the general welfare or general salvation. In a majority of imperial cities the Reformation constituted the first broad movement in which the urban classes acted vigorously as a group.

NOTES

1. Stadtarchiv Lüneburg, Br. 92. I am indebted to Mrs. Key of that Stadtarchiv for making this letter available to me.

2. Dr. Klaus Friedland, Archivrat of the Stadtarchiv Lübeck kindly showed me this letter. See *Hanserecesse von 1477–1530*, ed. by Dietrich Schäfer and Friedrich Techen, 9 vols. (1881–1913), Vol. IX (1913), Introduction, vii.

3. See the excellent studies by Bernd Moeller, *Reichsstadt und Reformation,* Schriften des Vereins für Reformationsgeschichte, Nr. 180 (Gütersloh, 1962), and Hans Baron, "Religion and Politics in the German Imperial Cities during the Reformation," *English Historical Review,* LII (1937), 405–27; 614–33. Other recent helpful accounts are those by Heinrich Schmidt, *Die deutschen Städtechroniken als Spiegel des bürgerlichen Selbstverständnisses im Spätmittelalter*

(Göttingen, 1958); Ermentrude v. Ranke, "Der Interessenkreis des deutschen Bürgers in 16. Jahrhundert," *Vierteljahrsschrift für Sozial- und Wirtschaftsgeschichte*, XX (1928), 476–90; Johannes Schildhauer, *Soziale, politische und religiöse Auseinandersetzungen in den Hansestädten Stralsund, Rostock und Wismar im ersten Drittel des 16. Jahrhunderts* (Weimar, 1959), a Marxist interpretation.

4. Bernd Moeller, *Reichsstadt und Reformation*, pp. 10–15; see also Otto Gierke, *Das deutsche Genossenschaftsrecht*, 4 vols., Vol. I (Graz, 1954); Wilhelm Ebel, *Der Bürgereid als Geltungsgrund und Gestaltungsprinzip des deutschen mittelalterlichen Stadtrechts* (Weimar, 1958), which has a thorough discussion and a helpful bibliography; Gerald Strauss, *Nürnberg in the 16th Century* (New York, 1966), pp. 69–71, an excellent summary.

5. Ernst Troeltsch, *The Social Teachings of the Christian Churches*, translated by Olive Wyon, 2 vols. (London and New York, 1931), II, 466.

6. Georg von Below, *Das ältere deutsche Städtewesen und Bürgertum*, Monographien zur Weltgeschichte, IV (Bielefeld and Leipzig, 1905), p. 16.

7. Erich Maschke, "Verfassung und soziale Kräfte in der deutschen Stadt des späten Mittelalters, vornehmlich in Oberdeutschland," *Vierteljahrsschrift für Sozial- und Wirtschaftsgeschichte*, LXVI (1959), 289–349; 433–76.

8. *Ibid.*, p. 324.

9. Hans Mauersberg, *Wirtschafts- und Sozialgeschichte zentraleuropäischer Städte in neuerer Zeit* (Göttingen, 1960), p. 109.

10. Schildhauer, p. 117.

11. Kurt Kaser, *Politische und soziale Bewegungen im deutschen Bürgertum zu Beginn des 16. Jahrhunderts* (Stuttgart, 1899), p. 13.

12. Georg von Below, p. 192.

13. Kurt Kaser, p. 188.

14. The city council of Nuremberg to Bishop Weigand of Bamberg, April 7, 1525. Staatsarchiv Nürnberg, Briefbücher, No. 89, folio 83v to 96r. I acknowledge my indebtedness to Archivdirektor Fritz Schnelbögl and his staff for providing me with a copy of this letter.

15. Julia Schnelbögl, "Die Reichskleinodien in Nürnberg 1424–1523," *Mitteilungen des Vereins für Geschichte der Stadt Nürnberg*, LI (1962), 78–159.

16. Klaus Friedland, *Der Kampf der Stadt Lüneburg mit ihren Landesherren* (Stuttgart, 1953), shows how a powerful city lost its autonomy in the sixteenth century.

17. Irmgard Höss, "Das religiös-geistige Leben in Nürnberg am Ende des 15. und am Ausgang des 16. Jahrhunderts," Miscellanea Historiae Ecclesiasticae, II, *Bibliothèque de la Revue d'Histoire Ecclésiastique*, Fascicule 44 (Louvain, 1967), pp. 17–36, has a helpful analysis.

18. See the excellent accounts of German Christian humanists by Bernd Moeller, "Die deutschen Humanisten und die Anfänge der Reformation," *Zeitschrift für Kirchengeschichte*, LXX (1959), 46–61, and Lewis W. Spitz, *The*

Religious Renaissance of the German Humanists (Cambridge, Mass., 1963).

19. Bernd Moeller, *Reichsstadt und Reformation*, pp. 38–66.

20. *Ibid.*, pp. 35–37, and Alfred Schultze, *Stadtgemeinde und Reformation* (Leipzig, 1918), pp. 27–38.

21. Hans Liermann, "Untersuchungen zum Sakralrecht des protestantischen Herrschers," *Zeitschrift der Savigny-Stiftung für Rechtsgeschichte*, LXI, kan. Abt. 30 (1941), 311–83.

22. Martin Bucer, *Martini Buceri opera latina*, Vol. XV: *De Regno Christi*, ed. by François Wendel (Gütersloh, 1954), Vol. XV bis; *Du Royaume de Jesus-Christ*, ed. by François Wendel (Gütersloh, 1954). For social conditions in Strasburg see the helpful volume by Miriam Usher Chrisman, *Strasbourg and the Reform: A Study in the Process of Change* (New Haven and London, 1967).

7

Some Last Words of Erasmus

MARGARET MANN PHILLIPS

NO CONFERENCE on the Reformation, surely, can avoid mentioning the name of Erasmus. I felt it a great honor to be asked to speak about him, though I also had a sense of danger; to confide this task to a mere biographer, not an historian, not a theologian, is to say the least of it risky, and I am fully aware of my limitations. Of course I have been interested in Erasmus all my life. And when thinking this over, I was comforted by the thought that Erasmus himself was cautious with philosophy, distrusted history, and was particularly repelled by some forms of theological speculation. Perhaps after all it would only be complicating things still more to approach him through these specialized fields? Standing as he does at the crossing of all the highways of thought and turning an independent eye on them all, perhaps he can best be reached from the biographical angle. Erasmus is Erasmus, and can only be studied as himself.

I was helped too by the memory of how as a young student I had sought out a teacher to guide me in the study of Erasmus' relations with France. My guide was Augustin Renaudet, and I mention him here not only in gratitude for the severe education he gave me, but because his work now provides me with a point of departure. All his life he returned to the study of Erasmus (this happens to everyone who is imprudent enough to embark in this direction) and his books constitute a close account of the daily life and thought of his subject, first up to 1517 (*Préréforme et humanisme à Paris*, 1916), then from 1517 to 1521 (*La pensée religieuse d'Érasmus d'après sa correspondance*, 1926), then from 1521 to 1529 (*Études érasmiennes*, 1939). His method is to weave an intricate tapestry from the complicated threads of

Erasmus' correspondence, shot through with references to his current writings and external events, thus giving a detailed picture of his life and developing relations with the world around him.

Renaudet went no further than 1529, the year when Erasmus left Basel for Freiburg. It may be that Renaudet stopped here because the later volumes of the Allen letters were still to come. Also he may have felt that the later years of Erasmus' life contained no new elements. He had developed in *Études érasmiennes* a theory that Erasmus was a *modernist* (in the theological sense) before his time, and he considered that the essential points of this attitude were defined between the publication of the New Testament in 1516 and the treatise on free will in 1524. From this time on, he wrote, Erasmus had neither the opportunity nor the desire to renew his opinions.

> [Erasmus] will sometimes be seen taking a step backwards—less, however, than some people seem to think. Already the necessities of a double struggle are turning him away from devoting himself to thought: a struggle on the one hand against the theologians and the monks whose bad influence in all domains, intellectual, moral and religious, he has not hesitated to denounce; and on the other against the Lutherans whose violence and prejudice displease his subtle moderation, whose new dogmatism offends his free Christian outlook, whose irrationalism repels his clear reason. Soon these necessities will absorb him utterly.[1]

There is no doubt that this double struggle loomed large in Erasmus' life. But I think his dealings with it in these years are worth studying, and the result is not negative. He was in a unique position and has remained in it ever since. It was desperately uncomfortable, but he could not be persuaded to abandon it. He never retired. Not for him a peaceful old age, but not for him either the ultimate defeat of denying his own principles. In fact, of all the names he has been called, perhaps the term of a modern writer "Erasmus the All-adaptable"[2] is the least true. These last years show him as supremely unadaptable to anything but the truth his own eyes see.

I shall therefore try to look at a part of those years which Renaudet left out, but not from the point of view which led to his conclusions. Taking it as axiomatic that one can never read texts enough, I have tried to reassess the attitude of Erasmus to the Reformation in the light of his last writings. They tell us perhaps nothing new, but they pinpoint those differences and shades which have been the subject of so much discussion and which can be seen more clearly as the years go on. Divergence of opinion is tremendous. One historian recalls that Goethe wished that the Reformation had been conducted by a man like Erasmus rather than a man like Luther, and adds "His wish was a vain one."[3] But it is a wish one often still sees expressed. A large (but diminishing) school of thought sees Erasmus as timid, drawing back when he saw danger, unfit to lead—and yet postulates that he would have wished to lead if he could. The truth of course must be that both Erasmus and Luther conducted the Reformation, the difference between their standpoints being that between two parts of a whole. Their objectives were so largely the same that any discussion must center on their differences.

It would be difficult in so short a time with such rich material to deal with the whole of this period of seven years. I propose to restrict myself to a few notes and documents of the years 1532–1535.

When one attempts to create a portrait of the Erasmus of this period, one is tempted to ask if he had outstayed his welcome. Would it have been better for his reputation if he had not lived so long? It is in these years that the note of querulousness and the sensitivity of the thin-skinned scholar become most apparent. After all, there is reason for this; the radiant days of what R. K. Chambers called "the golden age of Erasmian reform," the Utopian days, lit by the mirage of the classical landscape leading up to the heavenly Jerusalem—those days are over, and what is left is a darkening world.

One would like to dwell on the picture he presents, on his physical ailments now become chronic, his gout and something he calls paralysis as well as the stone; his discontent with Freiburg, once the refuge from the image-breakers and now a place of dirt, bad food and fleas—Erasmus stands at his desk (*stans pede in uno*) being bitten on ankle and collar; his constant attempt to find another home, the rivalry for him between Brussels and Besançon; his worries about money and the precarious nature of his resources, his acute sense of being under suspicion, having his correspondence tampered with and his name used by unscrupulous persons for their own gain.

Erasmus said treachery by a trusted servant was worse to him than a hundred books of Luther's.

One would think this quivering sensitivity had a pathological side and one would be reminded of the aging Rousseau, were it not that there is evidence in the letters from others that they saw him under constant attack. A letter from Levinus Ammonius in June, 1533, describes the situation of Erasmus as he saw it, holding on to his dual role as the restorer of classical learning and pure Christianity, threatened by the "marshalled regiments of sycophants" charging down on him with their tongues tinctured with poison and their slanderous books and accusations and blasphemies in their hands.[4] It reads like a page from Swift. Above all, says Ammonius, do not waste time on writing *Apologiae*. They have their interest, but these people are not worth it. Other letters of the time from anxious admirers express hopes that Erasmus will regain his old supremacy and confute his enemies.[5]

It seemed terrifying and unjust that these attacks should come from both sides, from the theologians of the Sorbonne and of Louvain, from the monks of Spain, through such mouthpieces as Stunica and Carvajal, Pio of Carpi and the rest, and also from the various camps of the Reformers. But it was highly logical. The complaints of both sides were identical. Erasmus had set up Scripture as the norm, and Scripture studied with the tools of the classics; he had made war on everything in the religious life of his time which had no basis in the New Testament; he had expressed a religious attitude diverging far from that of the Church of his day, and he was not willing, so they said, to accept the consequences and confess that his activities carried with them disorder and schism. Erasmus saw the matter very differently.

> This upheaval in the Church tortures my soul more than anyone would believe. . . . I was too true a prophet. . . . And now the evil is beyond remedy, and meanwhile the rulers of the world make endless war on each other. The monks attend to their own business, they have no wish to see Christ reigning in men's minds but they see to it that *they* reign; they particularly put their hope of victory in loud shouting before the people, which some of them are very good at. The theologians, through hatred of

Luther, condemn pious statements too, and those not invented by me, but handed down by the Apostles and by Christ himself. So by the stupid dishonesty of these people it results that many cling to the sect who would otherwise have left it, and many join it who would not otherwise have joined. But what stone have they left unturned, what do they not do, to force me, tired out at last with insults, into the Lutheran camp?... Yet no one has presented himself, Lutheran or Antilutheran, who can clearly point to any suspect doctrine in my books—though such hordes of them have done their best in this research. They bring along likelihoods, parallels, scandals, suspicions, and now and then a magnificent lie.[6]

· · · · · ·

What could be madder than these lunatics? I see clearly that if the Lutheran interest declines, there will arise such a tyranny of the monks that we shall long for Luther back again. And these are the monsters I am fighting against to my own ruin.[7]

So we have a picture of the old Erasmus sitting at Freiburg, as he said, like a snail in its shell, with the recriminations of both sides washing up to his door. His reactions are vigorous but they are not those of persecution mania, and if he had chosen the way of silence we should have lost some plain speaking.

In his dilemma, as has often been pointed out, he was subject to some strong temptations: to head a middle party; to put himself forward as an arbiter; to kill detraction dead by openly accepting the offers of Rome. Every biographer of Erasmus (or almost every one) is anxious to show that he was not the vacillating character he was said to be, and that his reputation as a trimmer was founded on misunderstanding. It is of course founded on the accusations of the Reformers. If Erasmus had been weak he would surely have fled for refuge to one camp or the other; as it was he stubbornly maintained his central position to the end. He ignored the urgings to head a middle party, which came from such enthusiasts as George Witzel, Luther's former protégé who had left the Reform movement owing to his reading of the Fathers and Erasmus; his two passionate letters survive. In the main Erasmus ignored the other temptation to become an arbiter and held aloof from the most tendentious questions of his time—such as the royal divorce.

There are involvements in these years which bear on the question of his integrity: for instance his relations with Cochlaeus (John Dobneck) who, when making his efforts to persuade James V of Scotland to ban Tyndale's translation of the Bible, sought support from Erasmus and obtained a letter of introduction for his messenger to the court of Scotland.[8] Was this one of the retrograde steps hinted at by Renaudet? Did it mean that Erasmus had thrown overboard the famous declaration of the *Paraclesis*, that the Scriptures should be translated into all languages, so that they might be within reach of all—the weaver at his loom, the plowman following his plow, the traveller on his journey? Luckily there is a later and still stronger declaration of faith on this point, in an appendix to the *Paraphrase of St. Matthew*, written in 1522.[9] Here it is not only the working man who is to have the Scriptures at his disposal but the prostitute, the pimp, the Turk, and there can be nothing wrong in everyone hearing the Gospel in his own tongue in which he was born; much better than to mutter psalms parrotwise without understanding. And in 1525, writing to Noël Béda, the syndic of the Sorbonne, he refers his critics to this appendix as a statement of his views.[10] It is hardly likely that they would have altered a few years later, and a look at the letter of introduction suggests that this side of the messenger's duties had not even been mentioned to Erasmus. In any case he would have held the same view of Tyndale as did More, who was engaged in controversy with Tyndale at this time.

The need for a widely read translation of the Scriptures was an article of faith which he shared with the Reformers, and we may well wish to clear him of rethinking on this important subject. Did he consider abandoning his position in another way, by accepting the offers of the Vatican and thus disengaging himself tacitly from his past criticism of the Church? No doubt the overtures were a comfort; to be offered the provostship of Deventer and know that he had friends at Rome who wished him to be made a cardinal, to be assured of the good will of the new Pope Paul III, was all probably balm to the spirit. But he had no illusions about the idea. He wrote wryly to Latomus in August, 1535:

Now as to my affairs, listen to something that will make you laugh. On the urging of Louis Ber, a distinguished theologian, I wrote a letter to Paul III. Before he broke the seal he spoke very honourably about me. When he decided in view of the future Synod to add some learned men to the order of cardinals, a proposition was made about Erasmus. But there were difficulties. My health was not equal to the task and my income was too small. For they say there is a decree prohibiting anyone from that dignity whose annual income is less than three thousand ducats. So now they are arranging to present me to Provostships, so that armed with suitable revenue I can be given a red hat. It's like dressing up the cat! . . . I can hardly put a foot out of my bedroom and even the thought of a donkey-ride is too much for me. This thin fragile body of mine can't bear any air which is not warmed. And they want to push a man in this condition to aim for Provostships and red hats. Still, I do appreciate on the part of the Pope both his mistaken view of me and his good will.[11]

Perhaps he was even glad to have an excuse. Rather than adopt such a material way of establishing his orthodoxy he preferred to write, and his positive proposals are contained in the letter mentioned to Paul III, and the *Book on the Unity of the Church* published in 1533.

These years at Freiburg give us a picture, then, not of a weakening hold on reality but of a stubborn resistance to pressure. By taking his own line in the teeth of every inducement to the contrary, Erasmus achieved a result he was far from calculating on—that of remaining "modern" if not for ever at least for several centuries to come. Each time he seriously put pen to paper now, the result was in the nature of a last will and testament. I should like to take three documents in illustration of this: the long letter he wrote to Bucer in March, 1532, the last exchange with Luther in 1534, and the *Book on the Unity of the Church.*

Perhaps on the whole rather little attention has been paid to the *Apologiae* of Erasmus, which most biographers (like Ammonius) seem to deplore, with the exception of Renaudet. Yet they are full of characteristic touches, and magically persuasive however much they may be special pleading. The letter to Bucer, like the *Purgatio* against Luther, is the final term of a long process of alienation. The case is a good example of how one *Apologia* breeds another. Erasmus' *Apologia* to the monks of Spain in 1529 had suffered a violent fate in

Strasburg; an extract from it had been reprinted with notes and letters by Gerald Geldenhauer (or Vulturius). Erasmus replied vigorously with his *Apologia* against the false evangelicals in November, 1529. This again provoked Bucer to a reply (Epistle of defence to the sincere followers of Christianity) in April 1530. The two were reprinted together with notes by Geldenhauer and this drew more protest from Erasmus.

His relations with Martin Bucer had steadily worsened since 1518 when the latter delightedly discovered, as he thought, an identity of purpose between Erasmus and Luther. His growing devotion to Luther led him away from Erasmus, and when he joined the Strasburg group of reformers and led them to adopt Zwingli's position as against Luther's, he took a step which would alienate the two still more. In 1531 the publication of the *Chronica* of Sebastian Franck roused Erasmus' ire, and taking it to be by Bucer he wrote in protest to the magistrates of Strasburg. In the final letter of this correspondence, written in March, 1532, he sums up his attitude to the Reforming left.[12]

What he had to face here was the allegation that his views coincided with theirs and that it was fear and fear alone which kept him from throwing in his lot with them. They were originally deeply in debt to Erasmus. If I may quote Professor Bainton, "one of the most curious aspects of the whole shift is that in many respects the radicals were the heirs of Erasmus, who saw the great abuse in Catholicism not as Luther did in the exaltation of man, but in the externalization of religion."[13] Perhaps it was this very fact which exasperated his feelings towards them. They utilized his Biblical studies and his attempts to redress the balance as against superstition and outward forms, to produce a doctrinal position which repelled him. It was no wonder that he was much more hostile to them than to Luther. Writing to Melanchthon in 1530, he had already spoken scornfully of Bucer as a *homo levis* and of Geldenhauer as his drunken and addlepated henchman.[14] The tone of the 1532 letter is hard. It answers point by point a letter of Bucer's, now lost, and, though Erasmus withdrew with apologies his suspicions about the authorship of Sebastian Franck's *Chronica*, there is little else of a conciliatory nature.

If the Strasburgers thought him insincere, he could richly repay the compliment. Strasburg is seething with scurrilous attacks and even his letter to Cardinal Campeggio pleading for peace has been reprinted and misconstrued. He has to state now perfectly clearly that their claim that he is secretly on their side is nonsense. "If that be true, I have never known myself." He challenges them to produce evidence that he shares their beliefs; as for their methods, he has always detested them. Above all, he has never felt as they do about the Mass, and he never will. Certainly he has said that simple folk should not be compelled to define how the Lord is present in the Eucharist; but this is emphatically not to deny the Real Presence. It is useless for them to hold out the hand and offer him a safe refuge if he will migrate to them; if he were sure they were doing Christ's business, he would be with them in three days, but they need not think it is fear of man which prevents him from joining them: "what I am afraid of is Hell."

This interesting letter expresses strongly Erasmus' practical side, his valuation of unity and charity as being marks of a Christian community. The Reformers are at loggerheads with each other, and this rouses deep suspicion. Even if he did not disagree with them, the prospect of being involved in ever new divergences would stop him. In his experience, these things make no one better. "People who join this sect immediately conceive a fierce hatred for those who don't agree with them—not a good proof of Evangelical spirit! . . . As for me, neither fear nor hope will induce me to profess anything I do not fully believe."

There was none of the uncertainty here which Luther saw in Erasmus. The exchange of letters between Erasmus and Luther in 1534 is similarly the culminating point of a long process of change, though it has usually been regarded as a kind of postscript to the main controversy between them. Many writers have followed the stages of the worsening of their relationship, and nothing shows the divergence of opinion on this debate more clearly than the fact that one critic will assume that Luther had the victory in *De servo arbitrio*, and that Erasmus' reply, the two *Hyperaspistes*, was a matter of pique at being thrust out of a position of leadership,[15] while others will praise the arguments of Erasmus and conclude that the embitterment of Luther was the result of a sense of failure. The difference of view seems to be a matter of temperament.

It is true that the acrimonious note of Luther at this time was a surprise to Erasmus himself and awakens speculation. It had seemed as if a certain neutrality had been reached. In his letters Erasmus is much more hostile to the reactionary party as represented by Béda of the Sorbonne and the Franciscans, and it seems to have been a cry from the heart—"If these people win the day, we shall long for Luther back again!" However misled and violent he considered Luther to be, Erasmus always recognized in him a fierce sincerity and a true devotion to religion. He remarks that much error is disseminated under Luther's name[16] and speaks with approval of his treatment of the Lord's Prayer[17]; just as a partial approval, with reservations, goes to Melanchthon's commentary on Romans.[18] Luther, too, had shown a certain broadmindedness in his preface to the refutation written by Corvinus to Erasmus' *Book on the Unity of the Church*.[19] At least he concedes that Erasmus' treatise was well meant, though the accommodation it proposes was impossible. But a few months later Luther's letter to Amsdorf stunned Erasmus with its bitterness.

The immediate cause of this latter outbreak was George Witzel, regarded by Luther as a renegade and one of Erasmus' party. Amsdorf had written to Luther advising him to ignore Witzel, who is merely the mouthpiece of Erasmus. It is Erasmus, compounded of ill will and ignorance, who should be attacked. "Luther's doctrine is heresy because it is condemned by Emperor and Pope, but Erasmus' is orthodox because Bishops, Cardinals, Princes and Kings send him gold cups. If there is anything more in it, may I die."[20] Luther's answer is a curious document. In it he agrees with Amsdorf on his verdict and encourages him to play David to Erasmus' Goliath. But if Erasmus is merely vain, why need one reply to him? "He will vanish in the end like smoke, with his vanity, if we leave him in the dark by our silence." This is not, however, what Luther proceeds to do. He attacks Erasmus on a number of grounds—his levity, his unwillingness to approach the main issue (though Luther himself had thanked him for doing so in the controversy on free will). Now he thinks Erasmus is willfully irreligious.

Not that he is ignorant of our doctrines, those of Christians, but consciously and with forethought he refuses to know them. Though he does not understand, cannot understand, what we teach against the synagogue of the Pope, those things at least which we hold in common with the Church under Papal rule he must know, since he writes a lot about them, or rather makes fun of them: that is, the Trinity, the divinity and humanity of Christ, sin and the redemption of the human race, the resurrection of the dead, life eternal and so on.

He hates all religions, particularly the Christian. He plays on words and hides behind double meanings. He intends to offend and then is shocked when there is opposition. He is Epicurus, Democritus, the mouth of Satan, governed by the Lamias and Megaeras he met with in Rome, a danger to the young, an enemy of the Gospel. These are allegations which are found in Luther's *Table Talk* of the same period and voice his final complete disillusionment in regard to the humanist he had first studied and appealed to, and to whom he once owed a measure of protection.

Erasmus' reaction is expressed in a letter written in April, 1534, when he too announced that he had no intention of writing a reply to Luther.[21]

I received a totally insane letter from Luther. Is not the man ashamed to lie so impudently? And he promises even better things. What are men thinking about when they commit themselves and their fortunes to a man so much under the domination of his passions? Nor does he consider how much harm he is doing to the cause which he pushes with so much zeal. George Witzel wrote to me twice, but from an unknown place, and so I did not reply. I knew he was meditating something against Luther, and I warned the man not to give way to his anger. I suspect that Luther was offended by my book on the Creed. . . . I have no mind to take issue with Luther. I prepare myself every day for my last; I am an old man in bad health, worn out by toil, dazed by mad and angry books. . . . Nor do I see what profit there would be in irritating Luther with publications. . . .

He thinks the present tug-of-war (a favorite metaphor) can never be resolved except by a summit conference. One thing he congratulates himself upon—having kept apart from all sects.

Why did Erasmus change his mind so quickly? His reply to Luther was written in the same month. Here perhaps the vicissitudes of illness are to be taken into account. Each spring Erasmus felt he was at death's door, but a sudden recovery gave him back his old resilience. The reply, which goes under two different titles, *Adversus calumniosissimam epistolam Martini Lutheri*, or more picturesquely *Purgatio adversus epistolam non sobriam Martini Lutheri*, was printed by Froben in April and reprinted five times at Antwerp, Cologne, and Paris. No wonder he remarked wryly to the ambassador to England that he was bombarded from all sides: the printers said no name sold better![22]

The *Purgatio* answers point by point the accusations of Luther's letter to Amsdorf.[23] Its atmosphere is almost playful in contrast to Luther's violence. The immediate circumstances of the attack are dealt with quickly and brushed aside; Erasmus replies suitably to Amsdorf's nonsense, but the interesting thing about his introduction is the assertion that he had never called Luther a heretic, had restrained Cochlaeus from violence, and if he had answered Witzel's letters would have advised him not to vent his anger on Luther. The tone of the treatise is not angry. It shows great psychological acuteness and returns often to the question of Luther's state of mind: his world is peopled with devils, Satans, specters, Lamias and Furies; he fights with shadows and sometimes he combines two grievances into one like a man seeing blurred things in a dream. How far is he balanced? It would not be worth while to reply if it were only a matter of counteracting wild insults, but Luther's attempt to persuade the world that Erasmus is using all his arts to ruin the Christian religion and bring back paganism has to be answered.

There are in fact two levels in this discussion: on the surface level of specific accusation Luther dwells on four or five points which Erasmus deals with at length. They are: first, that in his Catechism, Erasmus has attempted to disgust the young and repel them from Christianity, by giving an account of all the heresies, and no fundamental truths; secondly, that he admits the difficulty of interpreting the Epistle to the Romans (Erasmus comments that according to Luther's teaching there is no difficulty in Scripture, but all is open and clear to anyone who knows some grammar and has common sense); thirdly, that he remarks that Christ is hardly ever called God in the New Testament, nor the Holy Spirit either, and particularly adduces Peter's sermon on the day of Pentecost; fourthly, that he uses an obscene word, *coitus*, in speaking of the Incarnation; fifthly, that he writes frivolously and secularly, for instance in his *Methodus*, in speaking of the style of St. John (this is the confusion of two passages), and in the *Colloquies* and *Praise of Folly*.

It is remarkable, and Erasmus did not omit to point out, that some of these grievances are exactly those brought by the Catholics at the conference of Valladolid in 1527.[24] He can point to the *Apologia* against the Spanish monks as refutation. In fact here is a specific example of the identical criticism being used by opposite sides, and Erasmus can say to Luther:

> You approve of the attacks on me by the monks and by Pio of Carpi, but don't forget that they are the people who call *you* arch-heretic. You talk about me being a suspect author! You make me laugh. This from you is really too good. Who am I suspect to, if not to those who have condemned you utterly?

In the same way he can easily show up inconsistencies in Luther's attitude: for instance, in regard to the absence of the word "God" in reference to Christ in the New Testament. To Erasmus the assertion he makes is a matter of textual criticism; to Luther anyone who makes this assertion is an Arian denying the divinity of Christ. Erasmus says:

> But you are hoist with your own petard: you say there is no authority but in the text of Scripture; I accept the interpretation of the Church. All I have said is that the early Fathers were more cautious than we are in speaking of the divinity of the Holy Spirit, but they were bolder in their obedience to Him in their lives.

Since their time we have seen further: this "religious fear" ceased with the definition of the dogma of the Trinity. But our morals have not improved.

Underneath these specific points of debate there are vast areas of incompatibility. Luther sees Erasmus as unscrupulous in his treatment of truth. "Our King of Amphibology sits securely on his ambiguous throne." This question of interpretation of the Scriptures, for instance: the fundamental difference is between objective exegesis and devotional insight, but in the matter of authority of Scripture Erasmus obviously wants to have it both ways—he of all people had been the one to insist primarily on the supremacy of the word, on the paring away of all unscriptural practices and beliefs; now he says that Luther will accept nothing but Scripture pure and simple, while he admits the evidence of a deepening interpretation. This is a difference of character; in contrast to Luther's take-it-or-leave-it attitude, Erasmus sees these two facts—the immutable existence of the word of God and the growing awareness of humanity—not as opposites but as correlated and interpenetrating. Much has been written lately on his view of history,[25] and it must be accepted that he could not have an evolutionary conception or an idea of progress. But he often found truth in human consensus, and he believed that such opinions evolve.

Clearer than this is the other general accusation of Luther—that Erasmus leads the young into distrust of Christian truth; in fact, into paganism. An interesting point about the letter to Amsdorf is that Luther recollects the moment when he first began to be repelled by Erasmus: it was on reading the passage in the *Paraclesis* in which Erasmus asks the question: "What did Christ come to show us that was not revealed to earlier ages?" Taken out of context, this suggests that Erasmus is thinking of Christ only as a teacher, to be compared with other sources of wisdom—the Old Testament, the pagan philosophers—but of course Erasmus has no difficulty in showing that he does not, by asking this question, refuse to worship Christ as Redeemer. He has the same belief as Luther about the Redemption, though it is significant that where Luther uses the word *redimit*, Erasmus uses the word *restituit*; to Luther the emphasis is on the sin for which the price is paid, to Erasmus the emphasis is on the image of God to which we are restored. But all through Luther's letter runs the charge of paganism, of gibing at religions, all religions (as if there were more than one, comments Erasmus), of confusing sacred and secular, of using words like *fabula* for the drama of the Redemption, or *coitus* for the mystery of the Incarnation. In fact, of writing about religion as it if were not a sacred compartment, a holy of holies of the mind, but a natural part of daily life. Luther, so ready to take religion to the street corner, yet gibes at bringing to religious topics the use of natural reason.

Here it is the authentic Erasmus speaking, the voice of one who was so moved by admiration for Socrates, Plutarch or Cicero, that he could hardly bear to see them outside the Christian fold (saying for instance of Cicero, "I don't know where he is now, but I wouldn't quarrel with anyone who said he was among the blessed"[26]) : "In my opinion, it strongly confirms the doctrine of Christ, that it is not against the prophets and the promptings of nature—in this way it could be more easily accepted by Jew and Gentile."[27] For Erasmus, it is not blasphemy to say that the redemption of the world is like a drama; he might have said it was to ennoble drama. It is not blasphemy to use symbolic terms of human marriage to describe the Incarnation, and there is here, by the way, a very interesting and rather modern discussion of what makes a word obscene. It is of course a fact that there are really no human words to describe divine things, and for this reason we must not quarrel over language; he would have agreed with Montaigne who said "La plupart des occasions des troubles du monde sont Grammairiennes."[28]

This is not to say that Erasmus accepts the charge of ambiguity and of preferring to run through the world's heresies rather than state fundamental doctrine. What are the doctrines Luther accuses him of omitting? He makes a statement of faith.

I say: it pleased God that the world, fallen by the sin of Adam and Eve, from its original condition, should be mercifully restored through his Son Jesus Christ. To this grace all equally have access through sincere faith in Christ. Then, faith is a gift of God, which no one gives to himself, but it is to be sought from God. The material of faith is canonical Scripture, the Old and New Testaments, whose authority, emanating from God, I show by many arguments to be most certain and inviolable, worldly philosophy being set aside, and all human reasoning and experiment. This is the sum of the first part of the Catechism, in which there is no word that is ambiguous but constant and clear assertion.[29]

Apart from these fundamental things there must be ambiguity, and we must counteract this tendency of our speech by taking the whole of a passage into account, not seizing on words out of their context but interpreting them in the spirit of charity. Luther says he recalls the point at which he began to be alienated from Erasmus: "How much more humane is Erasmus, who was never alienated from Martin!"[30] Luther sees him as a Democritus, an Epicurus, a mocker of Christ.

> Of equal absurdity and craziness is what follows—about my hatred of Christ, my co-Epicureans, the metaphorical and insidious words in which I rage against the Christians, my double-tongued and insufferable way of talking, my intention of totally destroying the Christian religion—it would be tedious to go through the rest. You would say it was the disease talking, not the man.[31]

Luther in fact is crediting him with a sect (I never heard of this before, says Erasmus) not of Sophists and Papists but of Epicureans and their kind, who are so incredulous of divine things that they make a mock of everything. Erasmus admits that he likes jokes—and ruefully agrees that they didn't always succeed—but no one is without faults, and he would rather seem foolish than be morose and gloomy. To be always tragic, always on one's high horse, is madness rather than eloquence.

The piquant thing is that the favorite slander of the other side is that Erasmus sowed the seed of Luther's ideas. This will not suit Luther: he says it is an impudent lie; he can vouch for the fact that Erasmus is no Lutheran—he is only Erasmus (*Erasmus, tantum*). Actually, says Erasmus, this accusation of theirs is nearer the truth than Luther's assertion that the Anabaptists, Arians and Epicureans all stem from a few ambiguous words of Erasmus. "If this is really so, I marvel at the ingratitude of men. Not one of them thanked me!"[32]

There are a good many jokes in these pages, and Luther must have recoiled in horror at what Erasmus said about his violence:

"I, the Epicurean, if I had lived in the time of the Apostles and had heard them preaching the Gospel with the accompaniment of so much evil-speaking—well, I'm afraid I should have remained . . . an Epicurean."[33]

At the end he becomes serious.

> To speak seriously, if it is a matter of customs and ceremonies, there is much I would like to see altered, but through the authority of a council; if it is a matter of doctrine, I too might subscribe to some of these if I heard the public announcement of the Church. My mind is not satisfied by the assertions of Luther, however strong, since so much comes to mind which invalidates these assertions. Who acts against his conscience is building hell. In such a world-wide conflagration, let who will choose his own way. My aim will be to hand over my soul such as it is [*animacula*] to Christ my Saviour.[34]

What may well have shocked Erasmus in Luther's letter, though he never alludes to it, is the bitter ending expressing Luther's own sense of persecution.

> In other days it was a matter of great expense to canonize a dead monk. Now the easiest way to canonize Neros and Caligulas is hatred of Luther. Let anyone hate Luther and heap calumny on him, and it's done, he's a saint—almost equal to our sacred Lord, the servant of the servants of God. Who would believe that hatred of Luther could be such a powerful and fertile thing? It produces wealth for beggars and even for moles and frogs, it gives birth to prebends, dignities, bishoprics, it confers the reputation of learning on the very donkeys, it gives grammarians the authority to write books, finally it gives the crown of glory and victory for ever in heaven. Blessed are all those who have hated Luther. So shall the Scriptures be fulfilled: blessed are they who persecute Luther, for theirs is the kingdom of heaven. Blessed are ye when ye speak every kind of evil against Luther, rejoice and be exceeding glad in that day, because ye have a full reward in heaven, for so they did to the Apostles and holy Bishops, John Hus and his like, who were before Luther.[35]

It was perhaps Erasmus' turn to be shocked. The sense of dereliction which this passage conveys is very strong. Perhaps Luther did write it in one of his moods of depression, as Erasmus suggests. But the force behind it comes from a deep emotional source: in Luther's personal experience salvation has only come through the conviction of man's enslavement, and Erasmus' objectivity and assertion of freedom is destructive of the core of his inner life. Erasmus' lack of inner struggle fills him with a sense of injustice. Erasmus *must* be Mr. Facing-both-ways. To be an earnest student of the Bible and yet to feel that God inspired everything good even outside the Christian fold; to plead for a personal religion free from automatism and mimicry and yet to believe in the inescapable unity of the Church; to call for widespread knowledge of the Scriptures and yet require erudite understanding to interpret them; to put truth first and yet think it ruined, not supported, by the use of force—this in Luther's eyes must be vacillation or else hypocrisy.

As usual, Erasmus' reply pleased no one. The Lutherans could hardly be pleased; Melanchthon tried to prevent Luther from seeing it. But the other side thought it too mild. A canon of Augsburg suitably named Choler had written breathing fire about the letter to Amsdorf, urging Erasmus to answer it: if he does not, people will think he is afraid of his own conscience. "If you put up with this you are not the man I think you."[36] Choler's next letter grudgingly concedes that Erasmus has done something, but without sufficient punch.

> I'd like to sharpen up your pen. The first thing I disliked about your *Purgatio* was that you said you had never ceased to feel friendship for Luther. How on earth can you love Luther, by whom you have been loaded with so many frightful accusations and treated with such scorn? Besides, the man is the object of so many censures and bulls issued by Emperor and Pope, he is given up to the Furies, and never in his life did he write anything that was not stuffed with impotent and wild charges, huge lies and revolutionary howlings; come, my dear Erasmus, such a man as this, such a destroying agent, you never ceased to love? You needn't complain any more about your weak stomach, it must be pretty tough.[37]

Erasmus said he had preferred to deal with a light hand and to disregard those who pressed him to write bitterly. The violence he so much regretted was not to be mended with further violence, or the schism healed by the creation of any more parties. He was in full view now of the tragedy of his life, the division of Christendom attributed by so many to his own efforts to clear away dead wood from the Church. The *Purgatio* begins by saying that he would give his life, and ends by saying that he would accept the total destruction of his books, if either sacrifice could heal the wound. All he could do, however, was to try to speak for a dream of unity.

The book on restoring the unity of the Church was published in the summer of 1533. Its proper title is *De amabili ecclesiae concordia*, but the fact that it is often referred to as *De sarcienda ecclesiae concordia* has led at least one serious writer to allude to it as two.[39] It was analyzed and partly translated by P. S. Allen in *Erasmus, Lectures and Wayfaring Sketches* (1934), but the portion he translated or rather paraphrased is the short final section devoted to specific questions, such as the invocation of saints, images and relics, confession, the Mass, holy days, fasting. This comprises three pages of the *Opera* out of the seventeen covered by the whole treatise.[40] It is interesting to look at it as a whole and see how Erasmus envisaged the task he had been asked to perform. As usual, he did it in his own way and not in the way that might have been expected. First he wrote a learned and devout commentary on the 84th Psalm (83rd in the Vulgate): "How amiable are thy dwellings, thou Lord of Hosts." It is the description of a mystical Church, militant and triumphant, of which the entrance is faith (without which baptism is useless), and where, as in the Father's house, there are many mansions. It is not altogether false, says Erasmus, to talk as some do of an invisible Church. God alone sees into the heart and truly knows who belongs to that Church. These are his *Sileni*. But his concern now is with the visible Church, with its mixture of good men and bad, and how majestic it is. "The sparrow hath found her an house"; it is the humble Christian who builds his nest in the altar of God, and outside it there is no safety. There are remarkable things in this contemplation, with overtones that recall both the Fathers and the classics: "So immense, so capacious is the mind of man, that only God can fill it. . . . The mind of man is a thing of fire [*ignea res*], which even though weighed down by an earthly body, still has no rest until it soars up to its native home." Erasmus has a good deal to say about the horrors of heresy, keeping well to the past, in his comments on

"I had rather be a doorkeeper in the house of my God than dwell in the tents of wickedness," and so he goes on to the end, "Blessed is the man who trusteth in Thee."

Then he turns to the application of the Psalm to the present discontents. There are some notable things about his way of doing this. He is addressing himself plainly to the schismatic sects, but he adopts the diplomatic form of identifying himself with them and with all erring humanity by using the plural "we." This does not seem to be the ordinary use of the plural for the singular, but a more subtle method which is often misleading when used by Montaigne.

His reference to the Catholics are in no way a reversal from his lifelong campaign against abuses. His argument allows for all that is wrong in the organization and personnel of the Church; we can see much to condemn, but let each of us look at himself, and we shall find plenty to criticize there too. Pope and priest and monk may be unedifying, but so are workmen and merchants and lesser magistrates and the nobility and the princes. If the monks have gone back on their vows, how about our baptismal vow—have we kept that? We are in fact all in this mess together.

> We shall never come together as one unless we put all our hope in Jesus Christ our Lord and King, and look to Him alone. Where ambition reigns, or the love of money, or stubbornness, or blind favoritism or blinder hate, which makes us persist in sticking to what we have once said or written; when in deference to our own party we approve what we know we ought to disapprove, or from private resentment condemn even what is piously said—when every person is thinking of himself and the rope of the tug-of-war is stretched to the uttermost, then the affair cannot possibly be peaceably settled. Let us remember that it is stupid to hate the behavior of some popes and monks so much that we become worse than they are.[41]

This was plain speaking indeed, and an ingenious way of defending the Church. Wherever you look, he says, there are abuses, crimes, fraud and robbery.

> What is there left, but for each of us to examine himself and for all of us to fly to the mercy of Christ? ... Some vices are too slight for it to be wise to use harsh medicines on them. Some could be glossed over with less harm to religion than if they were violently attacked. Those which are too

serious to be passed over need a skilled hand, if we are not to be like the blundering doctor who applies a remedy and kills the patient instead of the disease. Some abuses have crept in little by little and should be removed in the same way, or borne with until a convenient time comes. The same skill should be shown in dealing with doctrine. Some with their shouts of *Heresy, Heresy, To the fire, To the fire*, while they put the worst interpretation on what is ambiguous and slanderously pervert what was piously said, are just inclining the general favor towards the very people they want to ruin. Again, those who are working under the plausible title of Evangelism to create a state of things diametrically opposed to the Gospel, are doing wonders to support the party which wants to suppress them. And so while these will not agree to any innovation, and those will leave nothing unaltered, the rope breaks and each side falls to the floor. Not the Church, of course, for she is founded on the Rock which is Christ and no storms can prevail against her. But I am talking of some who defend her cause with zeal but with no understanding.[42]

However, the situation is not Irremediable, if we will only stop blaming each other and honestly turn to serve God. Let everybody do his job properly and not spend his time looking at what other people are doing.

Here Erasmus turns to practical suggestions. Don't let us take it that everything has to be rethought and nothing accepted from the store of the centuries. Don't let us argue over words. Take the debate on free will, for instance, a thorny rather than a fruitful subject (and here he gives a swift summary of a middle position). Take the specific questions so often discussed: prayers for the dead? It would certainly be better to give one's money to the poor than leave it for prayers for one's soul, but those who hold this opinion need not disturb the simplicity of others. Let them rather see to their own generosity to the living. Invocation of the saints? Whoever does not agree to this, let him pray to Father, Son and Holy Spirit, but let him not rage against others who hold a different view; as P. S. Allen put it, "Christ loves simple souls and will hear our prayers even if the saints do not."[43] Images? Idolatry is a terrible crime, but pictures and statues are a kind of silent poetry; it would be good if all our houses were adorned with the picture of Christ. Relics? The best way to honor the saints is to imitate their lives, but, as St. Paul says, let each abound in his own opinion. Holy days? Their multiplication is troublesome, and it would not be a bad idea if those instituted by popes and bishops for the sake of indulgences were suppressed, like the Conception and Nativity of the Virgin; indeed, it might be better to suppress all that are not founded in Scripture, except for Sunday. Confession? If one is not persuaded that confession was instituted by Christ, it can still be kept as a useful custom and its usefulness depends on the way we handle it. Fasting? That is for those who benefit by it. Let those who eat tolerate those who abstain and those who abstain refrain from attacking those who eat. If Luther founded himself on Romans 5, Erasmus certainly founded himself on Romans 14! The longest section is on the Eucharist. It is right to eliminate superstition, to suppress private Masses and overuse of music, to avoid abuses of the sacrament, but let us keep the ancient and simple forms. Let it be enough for us to believe that Christ is in the sacrament, and leave the definition of substances and accidents to the council of the Church.

To sum up, three observations, it seems to me, can be made on the *Book on Unity*.

1. In essentials Erasmus has not changed his point of view since the *Enchiridion*. The same antithesis between the external and the internal pervades the book. It is the spirit which gives life; the spiritual quality of a sacrament is what makes the visible holy (and the reverse is magic); but without visible signs there is no sacrament. In this I think he did not disagree with Luther, but to Erasmus there was no difficulty about faith and works; he said clearly that faith is all that is required of the Christian, and it is the gift of God alone (for this he came under the censure of the Sorbonne). At the same time, from his essentially ethical and practical standpoint works are the outward and visible signs of faith, as if the whole life of man were a sacrament. The only difference between the *Enchiridion* and the *Book on Unity* is that the message is posted to a different address.

2. In the *Book on Unity* there is the same preference for simplicity as in the *Enchiridion*, the same dislike of intellectual jargon. He gives the simplest way of accepting the idea of the Eucharist, and adds:

"as for traditional terms like qualifications, principal and secondary merit, *de opere operante et operato*, these can be relegated to the category of human opinions, until the council pronounces a verdict or leaves them to the choice of the individual." All the distrust of medieval theology and the techniques of the schoolmen is still part of his nature. He is the pupil of the Brethren of the Common Life. I must apologize for making a judgment in these matters, but it seems to me than Father Louis Bouyer is right in thinking that this is less a matter of "modernism" in Renaudet's sense, a faith without dogmas, than of the *Devotio moderna*, a faith shown by active love.

3. Finally, the book was also one that could please nobody at that time. It fearlessly adopted an uncompromising compromise. Addressed to the Lutherans, it insisted that there was no safety outside the Church and called for toleration of tradition and practices harmless in themselves. Demanded by the Catholics, it took nothing back of the severe criticism of the hierarchy, the accumulation of superstitions, the unbiblical nature of many rites, and it called for toleration of a certain individualism. It was Erasmus' final answer to the pressure from both sides, and to the last temptation to range himself with the forces of traditionalism, as it were, with a tacit apology. What Professor Dickens says of More may be applied to Erasmus: "His recorded utterances make him a clearer martyr for the idea of international Christendom than for that of papal monarchy of the Church."[44] His slashing criticisms of the Church of his day could be combined with an unswerving belief in the unity of "the whole family in heaven and earth."

When in 1535 he wrote to the new Pope Paul III his letter summed up some of these things. It expressed his deep desire to see the Church at peace, his feeling that he had done what he could, his assertion that he was ready to suffer anything rather than give his support to any sect. He ended with the same plea for toleration of individual tastes and opinions, and for a general amnesty. Definition of doctrine can be left to the council, but it will not be necessary for the council to make pronouncements on every opinion:

for there are matters on which the Apostle Paul wishes everyone to be persuaded in his own mind, and there are some of which he wrote: if you think differently, God will reveal this to you also. In fact the variety of ceremonies does not break up the peace of the Church; there are opinions on which it is possible to disagree, without the destruction of peace between Christians.[45]

This concept of *adiaphora*, the category of things indifferent and unnecessary to salvation, is connected by modern historians with the name of Melanchthon, deriving from him and passing on to become one of the essential elements of the Anglican *via media*. It was certainly one of the points in which Melanchthon was at his most Erasmian.[46]

These notes on a few of Erasmus' last words are simple and incomplete, but they may serve to epitomize Erasmus' links with different trends of the Reformation. It is difficult for a layman (or laywoman) to understand why it should be said that his outlook was non-sacramental, when he found the doctrines of the Zwinglians so distasteful. Surely it is not conservatism but a deep conviction which is expressed in this unequivocal letter to Bucer.

In the *Purgatio* the full flavor of his opposition to Luther becomes apparent, the result not of differences on dogma but of a profound variance in their view of the world. The *Purgatio* and the *Book on Unity* both stress the idea he shared with Melanchthon, that the essentials of faith are simple and few, and the non-essentials many and various. With all the Reformers he held some beliefs in common, but one essential of Erasmianism would separate him from them all, the undeviating adherence to the ideal of a united Christendom.

Erasmianism is a pervasive spirit, recognizable wherever it penetrates (as J. K. McConica has recently shown in his admirable survey of the currents in early Tudor England).[47] It often acted as conditioning for more violent modes of thought, and sometimes what appears to be Erasmianism is a combination of elements foreign to it; for instance, I have never thought that Marguerite de Navarre could be called an Erasmian, though her blend of Lutheranism and quietism bears a superficial resemblance to the *Philosophia Christi*. It is an ideal which does not *fail* so much as fragment and reappear, as we find its pacifism among the Quakers, its toleration in the Church of England, its faith in the dissemination of the New Testament everywhere in Protestantism, its idea of unity in milieux both Protestant and Catholic. But in itself it is the personal amalgam of a subtle man who loved simplicity and thought a pound of dogma worth less than an ounce of charity.

He still does not belong to any cause. As Luther said, he remains himself, "only Erasmus"—not attached to the Protestant tradition but part of it inasmuch as it is part of the whole history of the universal Church. We might go further and say that if the Protestant tradition means the development of a changed emphasis in belief which could only flourish as a separatist movement, Erasmus was only unwillingly involved in it; but if it is taken to mean an essential aspect of the developing awareness and self-understanding of humanity, then Erasmus is one of the channels by which it was given to the world.

I think it is possible in our day to see that for all his nervousness and subtlety he was not weak in essentials, that the middle way is not necessarily a way of peace at any price. The element of permanence in Erasmus has always seemed to me to lie in his recognition of the human paradox: apparent opposites have to be reconciled, determinism and freedom, the simple man and the scholar, the paramount importance of the Christian revelation and the spirituality of pagan writers, the abasement and dignity of man. It was this sense of the two sides of the medal which made him so hate logic, or rather choplogic, and prefer common sense to the narrow definitions of the schools. To end with an adage: to have one's cake and eat it is not only possible, it is absolutely necessary if one is to be really human.

NOTES

1. A. Renaudet, *Études érasmiennes* (Paris, 1939), p. 189.
2. Erik H. Erikson, *Young Man Luther: A Study in Psychoanalysis and History* (London, 1959).
3. R. H. Murray, *Erasmus and Luther* (London, 1920), p. 353.
4. P. S. and H. M. Allen, *Opus epistolarum Des. Erasmi Roterodami* (Oxford, 1906–58), 2817.

5. Allen, 2842, 2651.

6. Allen, 2029.

7. Allen, 2868.

8. See Allen, X, 328–29.

9. Allen, 1255.

10. Allen, 1581, lines 740–42.

11. Allen, 3048.

12. Allen, 2615.

13. Roland H. Bainton, *Here I Stand: A Life of Martin Luther* (New York, 1950), p. 199.

14. Allen, 2365.

15. J. Mackinnon, *Luther and the Reformation* (London, 1929), III, 272.

16. Allen, 2780.

17. Allen, 2845.

18. Allen, 2818.

19. Mackinnon, IV, 106.

20. For this exchange, see Enders, *Luthers Briefwechsel* (Stuttgart, 1889–1931), X, 8–23.

21. Allen, 2918.

22. Allen, 2798.

23. *Erasmi opera omnia* (Leiden, 1703–06), IX, 1544 C.

24. See Marcel Bataillon, *Erasme et l'Espagne* (Paris, 1937).

25. P. G. Bietenholz, *History and Biography in the Work of Erasmus of Rotterdam* (Geneva, 1966), and M. P. Gilmore, *Humanists and Jurists* (Cambridge, Mass., 1963).

26. Allen, 1390.

27. *Erasmi opera omnia*, IX, 1552 A–D.

28. Montaigne, *Essais*, II. 12.

29. *Erasmi opera omnia*, IX, 1539 A–B.

30. *Ibid.*, IX, 1533 C.

31. *Ibid.*, IX, 1553 D.

32. *Ibid.*, IX, 1556 D.

33. *Ibid.*, IX, 1555 D.

34. *Ibid.*, IX, 1557 D.

35. Enders, X, 23.

36. Allen, 2936.

37. Allen, 2937.

38. Allen, 2961, 2970.

39. Murray, p. 340.

40. *Erasmi opera omnia*, V, 469–506.

41. *Ibid.*, V, 498 A–B.

42. *Ibid.*, V, 499 B.

43. Allen, *Erasmus*, p. 90.
44. A. G. Dickens, *Thomas Cromwell and the English Reformation* (London, 1959), p. 64.
45. Allen, 2988.
46. J. K. McConica, *English Humanists and Reformation Politics* (Oxford, 1965), pp. 4, 131, 160, 171.
47. *Ibid.*, p. 10.

8

Erasmus and St. Ignatius Loyola

JOHN C. OLIN

THE POSSIBILITY that St. Ignatius Loyola, founder of the Jesuits and perhaps the most pre-eminent figure of the Counter Reformation, was influenced by Erasmus and the broad current of reform humanism that swept Europe in the early sixteenth century is an interesting and attractive speculation. It has the merit, if any substance can be found in it, of overthrowing certain stereotypes and of casting fresh light on the nature of Catholic reform and on the interplay of ideas in this age of religious crisis. Even as a subject for inquiry it can lead to a new investigation and a new appraisal of several important aspects of Ignatius' life and thought. In view of the tendency to consider the Spanish saint in a manner quite routine and fraught with preconception, this will be no small service.

But what in the first place could give rise to the thought that there is a link between Ignatius and Erasmus? Neither personal encounter, nor literary reference, nor obvious similarity of character or mission suggests a connection. In fact at first glance they present a rather sharp and inimical contrast, and the disciplined, orthodox, and obedient spirit of the one seems almost the antithesis of the critical and undogmatic spirit of the other. And what specific mention one may find of Erasmus and his works in the sources relating to Ignatius indicate an aversion on his part toward the great humanist. Since Erasmus died in 1536, before the name or importance of Ignatius could have come to his attention, there is of course no reference to the saint in his extensive correspondence and literary work. Where then lies a relationship positive or meaningful enough to warrant the historian's consideration?

The answer to this may simply be that the historian, seeking to understand more fully the pattern of religious events in this age, pursues this theme for what it may be worth. His own orientation, his own interests, and perhaps some vague intimation of a bond may have suggested the question as a fruitful hypothesis.[1] Whatever the point of departure may have been, he would however soon confront the fact that Ignatius read, or at least began to read, Erasmus' *Enchiridion militis Christiani* in his early days as a student. With this golden nugget his exploration would begin. And at this point too our story may pass from the mere posing of the problem to the scrutiny of the circumstances and the evidence that seem relevant.

As is well known, Ignatius undertook serious academic work rather late in life. If his birth be placed in 1491, it was not until his thirty-third year in 1524 that he began Latin instruction in Barcelona and the long and checkered course of study that led eventually to a Paris master of arts in 1534.[2] What preceded these student years was his life as a Spanish caballero and soldier and then, following a great conversion, the months of penitence, prayer, and pilgrimage that inaugurate his religious career. The conversion took place during his recuperation from a battle wound he received in the spring of 1521, fighting against the French at Pamplona in Navarre. Reading of Christ and His saints, he resolved to serve our Lord and do great deeds, like the saints, out of love of God. This initially found expression in the desire to go to Jerusalem, and in early 1522 he set out from his native Guipúzcoa on his pilgrim's way. His journey took him first to the shrine of our Lady at Montserrat in Catalonia and thence to nearby Manresa where he remained for several months. He underwent there a deep religious experience, received, in his own words, "a great illumination in his understanding," and completed the transformation that his convalescent reading had begun.[3] At the beginning of 1523 he left Barcelona for Rome and Jerusalem. To his great joy he reached his destination, but the Franciscan guardians of the Holy Places rejected his plea to remain among them, and reluctantly he returned to Spain. It was now—in early 1524—"inclined to study so as to be able to help souls," as he expressed it, that he began his education in Barcelona.[4]

From there Ignatius passed to Alcalá in 1526, where he attended lectures in philosophy at the University which the great Cardinal of Spain, Ximenes de Cisneros, had founded fewer than twenty years before. Suspected however of being an *alumbrado*, he had serious trouble with the Inquisition and was investigated and confined. Finally to escape the restraints that had been placed upon him he went to Salamanca, but there too he aroused suspicion, and further trial and imprisonment were his fate. He then made up his mind to go to Paris in order to work more freely in helping souls and to study more effectively to this end. He arrived in Paris in February 1528, and there he remained until the spring of 1535. Such is the briefest outline of Ignatius' early years, his pilgrim years. I should now like to speak about several incidents during this time that bear upon our theme.

As I have already said, Ignatius at the outset of his studies read Erasmus' *Enchiridion*. The story is told by Pedro Ribadeneira, Ignatius' first biographer, a member of the young Society of Jesus and a man who knew the saint intimately in his later years.[5] Ribadeneira places the event in Barcelona when Ignatius was studying there in 1524–25 and tells us that Ignatius undertook the reading at the suggestion of some pious and learned men, including his confessor. As he did however, Ribadeneira reports, the saint "observed that the reading of that book chilled the spirit of God in him and gradually extinguished the ardor of devotion." Finally he cast the book aside, and he conceived such an aversion for the author that he never afterwards would read him, nor would he permit his works to be read in the Society.

This account in Ribadeneira is the most extended reference in the Ignatian sources to Erasmus. In fact, it is almost the only one—or more precisely, it is the most basic and comprehensive one, and what other references there are stand in close relationship to it. We shall refer to these as we proceed. At any rate the Ribadeneira text has given posterity the general picture of an Ignatius hostile to Erasmus and his spirit from the start, and from it, as from a well, is drawn the usual interpretation of their antithesis. Other factors indeed may be brought into play to explain their divergence, but Ribadeneira's account is fundamental and controlling.[6]

There are however certain critical observations that may be made about this key text and certain difficulties in accepting it at face value. This is said in view of a number of circumstances which we shall now discuss, but the one general critique that may be launched against this account is that Ribadeneira is describing essentially a very personal experience at second hand more than forty years after the event itself and that his description would seem to be a faulty and inaccurate ex-post-facto reconstruction. The lack of any really adequate corroboration for this particular story he tells makes him all the more vulnerable to the critic's knife.

For one thing, there is the problem whether Ignatius actually read the *Enchiridion* at Barcelona or a short time later after he came to Alcalá. The question is quite important, and it arises in the first place because there is a brief entry in the Memorial or diary of González de Cámara, an assistant and secretary of Ignatius in Rome, for February 28, 1555, to the effect that when Ignatius was a student at Alcalá he was advised by many, including his confessor, to read Erasmus' work, but that having heard there were "differences and doubts about the author" he did not want to do so.[7] González' statement has led some, including Marcel Bataillon and Father Paul Dudon, to believe that Ribadeneira erred in placing the incident he describes in Barcelona rather than in Alcalá, and for several reasons I am inclined to agree.[8] First, the state of Ignatius' Latin at Barcelona in these early years would have made reading the *Enchiridion* a very difficult, if not impossible, operation. We know from his autobiography that when he came to Paris in 1528 he had to begin his study of Latin grammar all over again, so shaky were his foundations.[9] Second, a Castilian version of Erasmus' treatise, artfully translated by a canon of Palencia, was published at Alcalá in 1526, the year Ignatius came to that university city, and he certainly would have had access to this edition.[10] In fact, he had more than simple access. He knew the printer, Miguel de Eguía, and his brother Diego, who, as Ignatius himself tells us, "helped him with their alms to support the poor, and maintained three [of his] companions in their house."[11] Miguel subsequently published several other works of Erasmus, including the *De libero arbitrio*, and in 1540 his brothers Diego and Esteban joined Ignatius in Rome to become members of the new

Society. The concrete situation here revealed would certainly seem to link Ignatius quite closely with the vigorous Erasmian movement at Alcalá. This possibility is heightened by the fact that Ignatius' confessor at Alcalá was a Portuguese priest by the name of Manuel Miona, himself an Erasmian and disciple of Bernadino Tovar who along with his brother Juan Vergara was a friend of Erasmus.[12] Indeed it seems very probable that the confessor Ribadeneira tells us urged Ignatius to read the *Enchiridion* was Miona, and, if this be allowed, then Alcalá becomes the place of the reading. And if Ignatius read the Spanish edition of the *Enchiridion* at Alcalá, then he was introduced to Erasmus under conditions that are extremely interesting and suggestive. In short, the strong likelihood that it was Alcalá begins to raise some fairly serious doubts about the whole tenor of Ribadeneira's account. And further evidence, I believe, only accentuates the suspicion.

My second observation about the Ribadeneira text concerns his description of Ignatius' reaction to the *Enchiridion*—it "chilled the spirit of God in him and gradually extinguished the ardor of devotion." I submit that the reading of the *Enchiridion*, and especially of its opening chapters and especially in the beautiful Castilian version, *suavizada y mitigada*, could not have had the effect on Ignatius that Ribadeneira describes.[13] This is not to say that the saint would have warmed to it as he did to the *Imitation of Christ* which had very deep and enduring influence on his life,[14] but that he would not have found anything really offensive in it and indeed may have found much that was meaningful and applicable to him. The fact that it was addressed to a courtier and soldier, a caballero, who wished to change his life, the fact that Erasmus used a military analogy and urged his reader to campaign as a soldier of Christ under the standard of Christ, the striking and lengthy reference to water "as a symbol of knowledge of God's law," which immediately recalls Ignatius' own account of his "illumination" at the river near Manresa[15]— all this in the very first pages of the *Enchiridion* could hardly have failed to impress the pilgrim student.

There is also a passage toward the middle of the *Enchiridion* that deserves special attention in terms of a possible influence on Ignatius.

The correspondence between it and a major statement of the saint is so close that there are grounds for believing that Ignatius may have borrowed from it.[16] I refer to the fourth rule that Erasmus presents as a guide to the Christian life—the rule that Christ is our only goal and that we must subordinate and direct everything to attain this goal.[17] In thought and in phrasing it is remarkably similar to the Principle and Foundation of the *Spiritual Exercises*, itself the classic statement of Ignatius' great rule of indifference or subordination.[18] Erasmus declares that whatever you encounter as you press toward your goal, "that you must reject or accept solely to the extent that it hinders or helps your journey," and he states that some things, such as health, learning, and the like, are neutral and that "of this last category, therefore, one should pursue none for its own sake, nor should he rely upon them any more or less than they help him hit the final mark." Ignatius' Principle and Foundation reads as follows:

> Man is created to praise, reverence, and serve God our Lord, and by this means to save his soul. All other things on the face of the earth are created for man to help him fulfill the end for which he is created. From this it follows that man is to use these things to the extent that they will help him to attain his end. Likewise, he must rid himself of them in so far as they prevent him from attaining it. Therefore we must make ourselves indifferent to all created things, in so far as it is left to the choice of our free will and is not forbidden. Acting accordingly, for our part, we should not prefer health to sickness, riches to poverty, honor to dishonor, a long life to a short one, and so in all things we should desire and choose only those things which will best help us attain the end for which we are created.

Whatever conclusion one may draw from this striking resemblance, one can at least, I believe, question Ribadeneira's text on the basis of it and aver that Ignatius and Erasmus shared a very fundamental attitude and expressed it in a very similar mode.[19] Rule four of the *Enchiridion* could not have "chilled the spirit of God" in the saint. The more likely conjecture is that it contributed to the formulation of his own thought in the *Spiritual Exercises*.

With reference to Ignatius and the *Enchiridion* Marcel Bataillon has another interesting relationship to suggest. He advances the notion that Ignatius' concept of a religious order reflects the dictum

Monachatus non est pietas found in the last pages of the *Enchiridion,* and thus he associates the organization and character of the Society of Jesus with Erasmus' criticism of the prevailing pattern of monastic life.[20] His argument rests chiefly on the fact that Ignatius suppressed choir or the chanting of the Divine Office in the new Society and that this bold step was viewed as a serious and even scandalous break with long tradition.[21] Many other features of the Society of Jesus, I believe, can also be assimilated into the Bataillon thesis—its emphasis on education and learning,[22] the long period of testing and preparation before solemn profession,[23] the mitigation of traditional monastic practices regarding fasting and other penances, its indifference concerning a distinctive garb,[24] the very name it assumed. Ignatius may not have been consciously inspired by the *Enchiridion* or any other specific work of Erasmus when he and his companions planned and organized their Society in Rome in 1539, but the fact remains that he did found a new and different order and that in a good many respects it does take into account the criticisms of Erasmus and others of the friars and the monks. In terms of his own vocation and spirituality he is saying something quite similar to the dictum *Monachatus non est pietas.* This may be one of the chief reasons why men like the Venetian humanist Cardinal Gasparo Contarini championed the new foundation and others like the anti-Erasmian Dominican theologian Melchor Cano vigorously opposed it.

To return once more to the Ribadeneira text, there is a third comment I should like to make in criticism of it. Ribadeneira tells us that Ignatius conceived such an aversion when he read the *Enchiridion* that he would not permit Erasmus' books to be read in the Society— *et passim in Societate nostra legi vetuerit.* This is simply not the case. Ignatius never enjoined such a prohibition. Erasmus was read in the Jesuit colleges and presumably by the members of the Society. The clearest indication of this is in a letter written by Father Annibal du Coudray to Juan Polanco, Ignatius' secretary, in Rome in July, 1551.[25] Father du Coudray describes the program of studies at the Jesuit college in Messina, a college Ignatius commissioned Jerome Nadal to establish in 1548. Like other Jesuit colleges, it was a trilingual college, and its curriculum is very important for providing a model or base for other colleges, including the Roman college, and for the later *Ratio studiorum*.[26] Du Coudray tells us that Erasmus' *De copia verborum* and his *De conscribendis epistolis* are used in the humanities class.[27] This testimony does not allow us to accept Ribadeneira's account.

After 1552 however there are certain references in the letters and instructions of Ignatius that do indicate that he was uneasy about the use of Erasmus' books in the colleges and that he would like to see them replaced by others.[28] In 1553 Polanco wrote to du Coudray in words to that effect, but he assured him that the present policy at Messina of using Erasmus was not objectionable and that they could continue to do so.[29] Finally it appears that in 1555 Nadal visited certain Jesuit communities, inspected their libraries, and set apart the works of Erasmus, Vives, and some other authors until Ignatius came to a decision about them.[30] From all this evidence we can only conclude that the Society did read and use Erasmus in their schools and that Ignatius up to the last year of his life permitted it, though in his later years—after 1552—he grew quite concerned about the problem. Ignatius' concern and caution, I submit, is reflective of a general attitude toward Erasmus that began to harden in these years and of a climate of opinion that was superorthodox, suspicious, and unbending.[31] Prudence became his guide in this matter, for he had no desire to see his Society falter under the burden of Erasmus and other controversial authors.[32] It had indeed enough problems of its own. There are no grounds, as far as I can see, for connecting this cautionary attitude with a reading of the *Enchiridion* almost thirty years before.[33]

It will be clear by now that I am extremely skeptical of the story Ribadeneira tells. I must confess that I see it as embodying an attitude toward Erasmus and a handling of the delicate problem of Ignatius and Erasmus more in keeping with the anti-Erasmian spirit of the Counter Reformation, that is of the time in which it was written, than with the actual facts of the case. The same prudence that may have guided Ignatius in his last years with respect to the use of Erasmus' works by the Society may also have dictated the inaccurate and unlikely story Ribadeneira relates. The fact that he concludes with a reference to the prohibition of Erasmus' books in the Society, erroneous though it is, would seem to bear this out. The Society had to disengage from any overt Erasmianism, and one might say its founder had to be placed in the other camp.[34]

There are however other reasons for rejecting the image of an Ignatius hostile to Erasmus and his spirit from the start and for calling into question the interpretation so general in Jesuit historiography of an antithesis between the two men. Thus at long last we may take leave of that basic text in Ribadeneira which we have been analyzing and proceed to certain other events and episodes in Ignatius' life that suggest a degree of affinity with Erasmus and the movement he represents. I do not mean that I intend to make Ignatius an Erasmian in the usual sense of that term, but simply to show that a "wall of separation" did not exist between them. In the absence of that wall lies the possibility of a meaningful interchange.

When Ignatius, because of the trouble and interference that marked the course of his studies and lay apostolate, left Spain and came to Paris in early 1528, he first entered the college of Montaigu. There as an extern he renewed his study of Latin grammar. Montaigu was one of the more than fifty colleges which comprised the University of Paris, and its history in this period is famous. It had been reformed by the austere John Standonck in whose hard days Erasmus had the misfortune (as he saw it) of enrolling there, it was attended by the young John Calvin who left with his degree on the eve of Ignatius' entry, and, more to our point, it was associated in the 1520s with the rigid scholasticism and antihumanism of its former principal, Noël Béda, one of Erasmus' most vigorous and intransigent enemies. Béda, then syndic of the faculty of theology at Paris, but still "master of the house" at Montaigu, was in the very midst of the campaign he had mounted against Erasmus and the French humanist Jacques Lefèvre when Ignatius arrived.[35] These scholars had been censured by the Sorbonne and denounced as clandestine Lutherans, and the reform humanism they represented was viewed with the gravest suspicion and alarm by many of Paris' foremost theologians. Béda was at their head. It would be remarkable if the attention of

Ignatius at Montaigu was not soon drawn to the issues and the personalities involved. What were his views? Where did his sympathies lie? Unfortunately the record is silent, at least in so far as any explicit judgment is expressed. But there are, I think, very clear indications that Ignatius cannot be ranged on the side of Béda and the antihumanists.

In the first place he left Montaigu after his Latin studies were completed and in the fall of 1529 entered the rival college of Sainte-Barbe for the philosophy courses which would lead eventually to his master of arts. The shift is interesting, for Sainte-Barbe was a more liberal college than the one he left and was quite penetrated by the new humanism which Béda so deplored. Its principal was a Portuguese, Diego de Gouvea, a Sorbonne theologian with an outlook very comparable to Béda's, but he was frequently engaged in diplomatic tasks for the Portuguese king, and the direction of his college during Ignatius' time was in the hands of his nephew, André de Gouvea, a man thoroughly sympathetic to humanist ideas.[36] There the Spanish humanist Juan Gelida taught, and there Nicolas Cop, whose inaugural address as rector of the university on All Saints' Day in 1533 stirred such excitement, was appointed regent by André in 1531. The college was decidedly more *aéré et ouvert* than the halls of Montaigu.[37] Whether this played any part in Ignatius' decision to move to Sainte-Barbe is hard to know, but two inferences, I think, can be drawn: 1. Ignatius evidently had no powerful attachment to the school of Béda,[38] and 2. he did not scorn the livelier intellectual atmosphere of Sainte-Barbe. From quite another standpoint it was a most fortunate decision. Living at the college, Ignatius was to share a room with two young students who had entered Sainte-Barbe a few years before he did. Their names were henceforth to be joined with his in the great enterprise that awaited them. They were a young nobleman from Navarre, Francis Xavier, and a young man of peasant stock from Savoy, Peter Faber.

Another incident that may well be indicative of Ignatius' attitude in these Paris years is a visit he paid to the famous Spanish humanist Juan Luis Vives in Bruges probably in the summer of 1529. Ignatius after he came to Paris made several trips to Flanders to beg his support from well-to-do Spanish merchants there. On one of these excursions he was invited to dinner by Vives who had returned to Bruges from England and his court post in 1528. Juan Polanco in his life of Ignatius gives us the account of their meeting and of a discussion they had on the subject of the Lenten fast.[39] Ignatius took exception to the views of Vives and argued with him, according to Polanco, and the biographer continues that Ignatius "began to have doubts about the spirit that moved him, and subsequently forbade the reading of his books in our Society, even those that contained nothing objectionable, in the same way as he forbade the reading of Erasmus." This account however, as Father Brodrick points out, "is not entirely satisfactory."[40] There are three reasons for such an appraisal: 1. because of classes in Paris it is most unlikely that Ignatius visited Bruges during Lent, as Polanco states; 2. it is hard to believe that Ignatius, a guest in the home of the learned and gentle Vives, would have argued the way Polanco describes or have come away with the harsh impression Polanco atributes to him; 3. Ignatius did not subsequently forbid the reading of Vives in the Society. The situation with regard to that problem is the same as in the case of Erasmus, with whose name Vives is generally linked in the references to his books. On the other hand Father Dudon reconstructing this interesting encounter at Bruges depicts the meeting of the two great Spaniards as the occasion for a very pleasant and stimulating conversation.[41] All the circumstances, apart from the Counter-Reformation moralizing of Polanco, lead one to agree. I submit therefore that the dinner party at Vives' home reveals Ignatius as not being hostile to the humanist movement, and I raise the point that it possibly—just possibly—may have had some bearing on Ignatius' decision to shift to Sainte-Barbe. Vives himself had once been a student at Paris, and he had come to reject with vehemence the scholastic dialectics that had such a citadel there.[42] It would not be surprising that he advised Ignatius to leave Montaigu and enter the more open and enlightened precincts of Sainte-Barbe.[43]

So favorable an interpretation of Ignatius' meeting with Vives is perhaps corroborated by this very interesting and significant fact, namely that the oldest extant copy of the *Spiritual Exercises* is in the hand of an English disciple of Vives, a priest by the name of John Helyar.[44] Helyar had studied under Vives at Corpus Christi College, Oxford. He later became rector of Warblington, the parish church of the Pole family.[45] He knew and wrote in praise of Erasmus. In 1534 he left England for religious reasons and came to the Continent, where sometime within the next few years, probably at Paris, he took the *Spiritual Exercises* under the direction either of Ignatius or of Peter Faber. His manuscript dates from this time.

Helyar's document must certainly be considered a link between Ignatius on the one hand and Vives, Erasmus, and Reginald Pole on the other. It may also indicate, as Bataillon suggests, a kinship between Erasmian spirituality and the Ignatian approach to piety and prayer.[46] In this instance the meditations on the life and passion of Christ, which comprise so major a part of the *Spiritual Exercises*, would undoubtedly have struck a responsive chord in Helyar. Indeed the whole moral and Christocentric spirit of Ignatius' discipline, as well as its fundamental interiority, would make, it seems to me, a strong appeal to the devout humanist. Here was a method, a way of personal reform, quite different from the external practices and the accessory devotions the humanists so frequently deplored. But regardless of how we may note the points of resemblance between the two spiritualities, the very existence of Helyar's manuscript affords concrete evidence of a certain compatibility. The spirit of Ignatius is not the antithesis of the spirit of Vives and Erasmus.

There is one last piece of evidence I would present at this time which casts light, I believe, on the relationship we are considering. It comes from a rather unexpected source, from a statement of the saint not usually associated with a very open or progressive image of him. I refer to his "Rules for Thinking with the Church," an appendix of the *Spiritual Exercises*.[47] According to the best authorities, these eighteen concise rules were drafted during Ignatius' Paris years, and Father Dudon makes a very convincing case that they were inspired by the decrees of the Council of Sens, held at Paris in 1528, and by the writings of Josse Clichtove who was active at the Council and more generally in the defense of Catholic doctrine against the Lutheran teachings.[48] Nearly all admit that they are specifically anti-Protestant, and indeed their whole thrust is to inculcate obedience to the Church and respect for traditional Catholic observances. Several of the rules—such as number six, praising the veneration of the relics of the saints, or number seven, praising the precepts concerning fast and abstinence—would seem to dissociate Ignatius from some of Erasmus' sharpest criticism, but too much, I believe, should not be made of this. Above all these "Rules" must not be read as a kind of anti-Erasmian or anti-humanist manifesto. The clearest proof of this is rule eleven in which Ignatius urges us "to praise both positive and scholastic theology." In that simple, unpretentious rule, the full import of which may be missed by those who fail to read it in the context of its times, the saint accepts with one decisive gesture the heart of Christian humanism—the renewal of theology through a return to Holy Scripture and the Fathers. He combines this, it is true, with the acceptance of a sound scholasticism, based above all on St. Thomas. By glaring omission he rejects the nominalism of Montaigu, Béda, and the Sorbonne. In short, he finds his footing amid the swirling intellectual currents of his day, and he lays the base for a creative and constructive synthesis. It will not be amiss to recall that after he finished his arts course at Sainte-Barbe Ignatius studied theology at the Dominican convent on the rue Saint-Jacques.[49] It was in this famous school that under Pierre Crockaert a revival of St. Thomas had begun in the early years of the century. Ignatius' position then as reflected in rule eleven associates him more with the theological approach of Cajetan or Contarini than with the antihumanism of Béda, and indeed it will come as no surprise to discover that when the saint finally came to Rome at the end of 1537 he found in Cardinal Contarini the champion of his apostolate and his new Society.[50]

The "Rules" offer still another indication, I believe, of the moderate and balanced attitude of Ignatius during these Paris years. Protestantism had become a serious problem and a threat in France, though the crisis did not appear grave enough in the eyes of Ignatius and his companions to deter them from their plan—Ignatius' original desire —to go to the East to evangelize the Turks. They solemnly vowed to do precisely that in a chapel on Montmartre in August 1534. This intention and vocation in themselves are very interesting facts, given all that was happening in Christian Europe in these very days. But just as interesting is the tone of rules fourteen through seventeen. Ignatius counsels us to be careful of the way we discuss the controversial questions of faith and grace. In these injunctions he is truly the master of calm, cooling, and deliberate understatement. Would that both sides had listened to him! And in rule seventeen he states:

> Also in our discourse we ought not to emphasize the doctrine that would destroy free will. We may therefore speak of faith and grace to the extent that God enables us to do so, for the greater praise of His Divine Majesty. But, in these dangerous times of ours, it must not be done in such a way that good works or free will suffer any detriment or be considered worthless.

This position, I submit, in tone and in substance is remarkably close to the position of Erasmus. I do not say it was borrowed from him, but I do hold the view that it indicates, as do so many other comparable instances, that Ignatius was not so far from the fundamental spirit of Erasmus as we are often led to believe.[51]

NOTES

1. The question of course is not entirely original. Henri Brémond in the opening pages of his *Histoire littéraire du sentiment religieux en France depuis la fin des guerres de religion jusqu'à nos jours* (11 vols.; Paris, 1916–33), I, saw a close relationship between the early Jesuits and the tradition of Christian humanism, and Marcel Bataillon in *Erasme et l'Espagne* (Paris, 1937), pp. 229–31, strongly suggests the influence of Erasmus on Ignatius. I mention these two authors in particular as directing my own thought to the problem. There is also some literature on the subject, as I soon discovered, notably R. G. Villoslada, s.j., "San Ignacio de Loyola y Erasmo de Rotterdam," *Estudios eclesiasticos*, XVI (1942), 235–64, 399–426, and XVII (1943), 75–103, a lengthy analysis taking issue with Bataillon, and M. Olphe-Galliard, s.j., "Erasme et Ignace de Loyola," *Revue d'ascétique et de mystique*, XXXV (1959), 337–52, an excellent bibliographical article. Father Villoslada's study, amplified and revised, has been published in book form, *Loyola y Erasmo, dos almas, dos epocas* (Madrid, 1965), though I have not used or cited this work.

2. On the life of St. Ignatius, see James Brodrick, s.j., *The Origin of the Jesuits* (New York, 1940) and *Saint Ignatius Loyola, the Pilgrim Years, 1491–1538* (New York, 1956), and Paul Dudon, s.j., *St. Ignatius of Loyola*, trans. William J.

Young, S.J. (Milwaukee, 1949). Ignatius' most important autobiography "as told to Luis González de Cámara" may be found in *St. Ignatius' Own Story*, trans. William J. Young, S.J. (Chicago, 1956). The earliest *vitae* and the basic sources for his life are in *Fontes narrativi de S. Ignatio de Loyola* (4 vols. Rome, 1943–65), a section of the voluminous *Monumenta Historica Societatis Jesu*. There are two very useful bibliographies for Ignatius: Jean-François Gilmont, S.J., and Paul Daman, S.J., *Bibliographie ignatienne* (1894–1957) (Paris-Louvain, 1958), and I. Iparraguirre, S.J., *Oriéntaciones bibliograficas sobre San Ignacio de Loyola* (2nd ed.; Rome, 1965).

3. On the Manresa experience, see especially *St. Ignatius' Own Story*, Chap. 3, and Hugo Rahner, S.J., *The Spirituality of St. Ignatius Loyola*, trans.William J. Young, S.J. (Westminster, Md., 1953).

4. *St. Ignatius' Own Story*, p. 36.

5. In his *Vita Ignatii Loiolae*, Book I, Chap. XIII, a work written in 1567–69 and first published in Naples in 1572. There were many subsequent editions, and Ribadeneira himself translated it into Spanish and first published this version in Madrid in 1583. The critical edition of the Latin and Spanish texts is in *Fontes narrativi de S. Ignatio de Loyola*, IV, pp. 172–75 of which give the account of the reading.

Ribadeneira (1526–1611) met Ignatius in Rome in 1540, and he entered the Society of Jesus that same year, its founding year, an extremely young novice indeed. His studies occupied the next several years and took him to Paris in 1542 and to Padua in 1545–49. He taught in Palermo in 1549–52 and was made principal of the new Germanicum in Rome in 1552. He was one of Ignatius' closest associates in the last years of the saint's life. See *Enciclopedia Universal Ilustrada Europeo-Americana*, LI, 292–93, and also Jean-François Gilmont, S.J., *Les écrits spirituels des premiers Jésuits* (Rome, 1961), pp. 32–33, 269–76.

6. This is quite clear, I believe, from Father Villoslada's articles in *Estudios eclesiásticos* and from Father Brodrick's *Saint Ignatius Loyola, the Pilgrim Years*, where (on pp. 156–63) Ribadeneira's account is followed and much is made of the contrast between the two men. Father Brodrick's sketch of Erasmus in these pages, I might add, is a caricature.

7. *Fontes narrativi de S. Ignatio de Loyola*, I, 669. There is another entry substantially the same in González' Memorial, *ibid.*, I, 585, but this was made as an annotation in Portuguese many years later. The original entry of 1555, it will be noted, is a much earlier text than Ribadeneira's and actually dates from Ignatius' own lifetime (he died July 31, 1556). See Gilmont, *op. cit.*, pp. 37–38.

8. Bataillon, *op. cit.*, pp. 229–30, and Dudon, *op. cit.*, p. 107. Dudon makes reference to Polanco rather than to Ribadeneira, *i.e.* to Juan Polanco, *Vita Ignatii Loiolae et rerum Societatis Jesu historia*, where substantially the same story is told about Ignatius reading the *Enchiridion* in Barcelona. See *Fontes narrativi*,

II,' 543. Polanco however wrote his *Vita* in 1574 and took the story about Ignatius and the *Enchiridion* from Ribadeneira.

9. *St. Ignatius' Own Story*, p. 52.

10. On the Castilian version of the *Enchiridion*, see Bataillon, *op. cit.*, pp. 205ff.

11. *St. Ignatius' Own Story*, p. 41. See also Villoslada, *op. cit.*, XVI, 255–56, 260–61.

12. Bataillon, *op. cit.*, p. 230. González de Cámara specifically mentions Miona as the confessor who recommended the reading of the *Enchiridion*, in *Fontes narrativi*, I, 585. Miona entered the Society of Jesus in 1545.

13. Father Villoslada, *op. cit.*, XVI, 238, 241ff. frankly acknowledges this— an admission, in my judgment, which seriously undercuts his thesis.

14. Joseph de Guibert, S.J., *The Jesuits, Their Spiritual Doctrine and Practice*, trans. William J. Young, S.J. (Chicago, 1964), pp. 155–56.

15. *St. Ignatius' Own Story*, pp. 23–24.

16. Father Villoslada also acknowledges this, although he himself does not hold that Ignatius borrowed it. See his work, XVI, 244–48. The statement of H. R. Trevor-Roper in his essay on Erasmus that "Loyola himself had read Erasmus' *Enchiridion*, and he based his *Spiritual Exercises* fundamentally upon it," in *Historical Essays* (New York, 1966), p. 57, is of course a gross exaggeration.

17. Erasmus, *The Enchiridion*, trans. Raymond Himelick (Bloomington, Ind., 1963), pp. 94–101.

18. St. Ignatius, *The Spiritual Exercises*, trans. Anthony Mottola (New York, 1964), pp. 47–48. The rule is stated elsewhere at key places in the *Exercises*, e.g. the third class of men, p. 78, the second mode of humility, p. 82, the election, pp. 82–83.

It is not possible to date the *Spiritual Exercises* or the composition of its various parts with precision. The book as we have it today developed in the period between Manresa (1522) and the time Ignatius left Paris (1535). The "first week" was substantially complete when the saint was at Alcalá, though we do not know if the Principle and Foundation had then been drafted. That latter rule probably dates from his Paris years, though that in itself does not rule out the actual origin of it at Alcalá. On the earliest texts of the *Spiritual Exercises*, see Gilmont, *op. cit.*, Chap. II.

19. For another example on the part of Erasmus of an Ignatian-like spirit of indifference toward created things I should like to call attention to his colloquy, "The Well-to-do Beggars," first published in 1524. There are also a few points in that colloquy that suggest the young Society of Jesus. See Erasmus, *The Colloquies*, trans. Craig R. Thompson (Chicago, 1965), pp. 203–17.

20. Bataillon, *op. cit.*, p. 230.

21. *Ibid.*, p. 747. It was one of the main points raised by Cardinal Ghinucci in his objections to the plan of the new Society when papal approval was being

discussed in 1540, and it continued to be a major point at issue among those who were hostile to the early Jesuits. After Gian Pietro Carafa (with whom Ignatius had long had serious differences) became Pope Paul IV in 1555, he imposed the obligation of choir, though it was subsequently revoked.

22. In this regard I should like to call attention to Ignatius' famous Letter to the Fathers and Brothers of Coimbra, May 7, 1547, reprinted in *Readings in Church History*, ed. Colman J. Barry, O.S.B. (Westminster, Md., 1965), II, 112–19.

23. This feature can be said to be especially significant in view of Erasmus' persistent criticism that young men were hustled into the monastic life before they had the chance to make a free and fair decision. One might also note the emphasis Ignatius gives in the *Spiritual Exercises* to the election, i.e. to the "wise and good" choice of a way of life. It is the very focal point of his discipline.

24. Another very significant feature in view of a criticism Erasmus constantly makes. See for instance "The Well-to-do Beggars."

25. *Monumenta Historica Societatis Jesu, Litterae Quadrimestres*, I (Madrid, 1897), 349–58.

26. Allan P. Farrell, S.J., *The Jesuit Code of Liberal Education* (Milwaukee, 1938), Chaps. I and II. On the character of Jesuit education, so thoroughly humanist, see François de Dainville, S.J., *La naissance du l'humanisme moderne* (Paris, 1940), Vol. I: *Les Jésuits et l'humanisme* (the only volume published of this interesting work).

27. Du Coudray also says that Nadal (who was the rector at Messina) thought it possible to use Lorenzo Valla in the advanced grammar class and that in dialectics where Aristotle was studied the works either of George of Trebizond or Jacques Lefèvre were used. The college had a remarkably humanist orientation indeed.

28. The pertinent texts are quoted and discussed in Villoslada, *op. cit.*, XVII, 88–100. Villoslada readily admits that Erasmus was widely used in the Jesuit colleges and that "Saint Ignatius never dictated to the Company a law or general decree against Erasmian books" (p. 96).

29. *Ibid.*, XVII, 92. Brodrick, *Saint Ignatius Loyola, the Pilgrim Years*, p. 228, also quotes this letter, and he concludes that "Ignatius never forbade the reading of Erasmus and Vives outright, but merely discountenanced it."

30. Villoslada, *op. cit.*, XVII, 96–97, and Bataillon, *op. cit.*, p. 587.

31. A situation signaled and described in *ibid.*, Chap. XIII: *L'érasmisme condamné*. A kind of climax was reached in the Index of Paul IV in 1558 which held Erasmus to be a heretic *primae classis* and condemned all his works (*ibid.* p. 760). The Spanish Index of 1559 was a bit less draconian, but it prohibited a good portion of his writing, including the *Enchiridion* (*ibid.*, pp. 762–63).

32. The only reference to Erasmus in Ribadeneira's *Vita Ignatii Loiolae* other than the one we have been discussing is a brief remark toward the end of his work (Book V, Chap. X) that Ignatius did not want the Society to read

authors like Erasmus, *dubii ac suspecti*, and Ribadeneira adds that Ignatius was of this opinion "long before they were censured by the Apostolic See." The chapter where this information is given us is entitled "Prudence in Spiritual Matters." *Fontes narrativi*, IV, 858–61.

33. Polanco, who in his *Vita Ignatii Loiolae* repeats substantially the same story Ribadeneira tells about Ignatius and the *Enchiridion* (see n. 8), adds however that Ignatius prohibited the reading of Erasmus in the Society "when he afterwards became still better acquainted with the spirit of Erasmus." *Fontes narrativi*, II, 543. Both authors are in error about the prohibition, but at least Polanco does not connect it with the early reading of the *Enchiridion*.

34. This criticism of Ribadeneira is of course quite aside from the fact that the author was born only in 1526, the year Ignatius came to Alcalá. His story at best could only be based on a later recollection.

It need hardly be pointed out that our criticism of Ribadeneira in this instance also applies to Polanco and, for that matter, to Gian Pietro Maffei, whose life of Ignatius, first published in 1585, follows Polanco.

35. Besides the biographies of Ignatius by Brodrick and Dudon, the following articles are excellent on Ignatius' Paris years: H. Bernard-Maître, s.j., "Les fondateurs de la Compagnie de Jésus et l'humanisme parisien de la Renaissance," *Nouvelle Revue Théologique*, 72 (1950), 811–23; I. Rodriguez-Grahit, "Ignace de Loyola et le college Montaigu. L'influence de Standonck sur Ignace," *Bibliothèque d'Humanisme et Renaissance*, XX (1958), 388–401; and Robert Rouquette, s.j., "Ignace de Loyola dans le Paris intellectual du XVIe siècle," *Études*, 290 (1956), 18–40.

36. On the two Gouveas, see Marcel Bataillon, *Études sur le Portugal au temps de l'humanisme* (Coimbra, 1952), pp. 109–29.

37. Bernard-Maître, *op. cit.*, pp. 821–23, 830.

38. Rouquette, *op. cit.*, p. 30.

39. *Fontes narrativi*, II, 557–58. The text is quoted and discussed also in Villoslada, *op. cit.*, XVII, 82–85, and Broderick, *Saint Ignatius Loyola, the Pilgrim Years*, pp. 226–27. Polanco's *Vita Ignatii Loiolae*, which was written in 1574, is our only source for this story.

40. Brodrick, *Saint Ignatius Loyola, the Pilgrim Years*, p. 227.

41. Dudon, *op. cit.*, pp. 133–34.

42. Notably in his *In Pseudo-dialecticos* of 1520. See Bataillon, *Erasme et l'Espagne*, pp. 18–19, 108–09, *et passim*.

43. I presume that Vives knew the Gouveas as well as the humanist scholar Juan Gelida, a Valencian like himself. It may be interesting to investigate these relationships.

As a postscript to the story of Ignatius' visit to the home of Vives, I might note that Ignatius also paid a visit to the home of the Portuguese humanist Damiâo de Gois in Padua ca. 1537. It appears to have been occasioned by an argument that Ignatius' companion Simon Rodriguez had with Gois. Ignatius came to apologize. See Bataillon, *Études sur le Portugal*, p. 255, n. 1, and Elisabeth Feist Hirsch, *Damião de Gois, the Life and Thought of a Portuguese Humanist*, 1502–1574 (The Hague, 1967), p. 96.

44. Helyar's text is in *Monumenta Ignatiana, Exercitia Spiritualia* (Madrid, 1919), pp. 624–48. On Helyar, see Herbert Thurston, s.j., "The First Englishman to Make the *Spiritual Exercises*," *The Month*, 142 (1923), 336–47, and Henry de Vocht, "John Helyar, Vives' Disciple," *Humanistica Lovaniensia*, IV (1934), 587–608.

45. Joseph Crehan, s.j., "Saint Ignatius and Cardinal Pole," *Archivum Historicum Societatis Iesu*, XXV (1956), 73–75.

46. Bataillon, *Erasme et l'Espagne*, pp. 631–32. See also de Guibert, *op. cit.*, pp. 164–65. Father de Guibert notes "the undeniable similarity in many features between the ideas of Ignatius and those of these spiritual humanists," i.e. Erasmus, Vives, Lefèvre, and he feels that this similarity is due to a common source, namely the *Devotio moderna*. Indeed I believe this is a very large part of the story. With regard to the influence of the *Devotio* on Ignatius I should like to call attention to I. Rodriguez-Grahit, "La *Devotio moderna* en Espagne et l'influence française," *Bibliothèque d'Humanisme et Renaissance*, XIX (1957), 489–95.

47. St. Ignatius, *The Spiritual Exercises* (edition cited), pp. 139–42.

48. Dudon, *op. cit.*, pp. 146, 457–62.

49. *Ibid.*, pp. 143–45, and Rouquette, *op. cit.*, pp. 31–32.

50. See the extremely interesting article by Angel Suquia, "Las reglas para sentir con la iglesia en la vida y en las obras del Cardenal Gaspar Contarini (1483–1542)," *Archivum Historicum Societatis Iesu*, XXV (1956), 380–95.

51. Since I wrote and delivered the above paper two recently published studies very relevant to this theme have come to my attention, and I should like to take note of them at least in a final postscript. They are Marcel Bataillon, "D'Erasme à la Compagnie de Jésus," *Archives de sociologie des religions*, XXIV (1967), 57–81, and H. O. Evennett, *The Spirit of the Counter-Reformation*, ed. John Bossy (Cambridge, 1968). Bataillon's article, elaborating references to St. Ignatius and the young Society in his *Erasme et l'Espagne*, particularly the thesis that the Society of Jesus was a major departure from monastic tradition and reflected the Erasmian dictum *Monachatus non est pietas*, takes up many of the points I have discussed and is generally corroborative of the view I have developed. He gives, however, another and most interesting explanation for the drafting of the "Rules for Thinking with the Church." He sees them as an affirmation of orthodoxy occasioned by the need to protect the young Society in the face of the opposition it met from Cardinals Ghinucci and Guidiccioni when papal approval was being sought in 1539–40. Indeed this may in part be the case, but the significance of the "Rules" as well as their scope, I believe,

extends far beyond this single though very critical occasion. Evennett's work (the posthumous publication of his Birkbeck Lectures at the University of Cambridge in 1959) covers a much larger subject of course than my or Bataillon's theme, but it lays great stress on the role of Ignatius and his Society in the development of Catholic reform, and it discusses at length the character of Ignatian spirituality (Chap. III) and the features of the new religious Order (Chap. IV). Evennett places both in the context of their times, linking Ignatius' spiritual formation to the influence of the *Devotio moderna* and the Society to contemporary currents and needs. He treats the specific question of Erasmus' influence rather gingerly (pp. 54–55, 63–64, 74–77), but the whole approach and tenor of his study tend to substantiate the general view I have expressed.

Recent Studies of Luther and the Reformation

LEWIS W. SPITZ

"La bibliographie est le vestibule de la science."

General Histories of the Reformation:

Bergendoff, Conrad, *The Church of the Lutheran Reformation: A Historical Survey of Lutheranism* (St. Louis, 1967).
  A survey of Lutheran history relating "the church of the Lutheran Reformation to the church catholic of all ages."
Chadwick, Owen, *The Reformation* (Baltimore, 1964).
  This third volume of the Pelican History of the Church is a lively account drawing heavily on the English church for illustrative incidents.
Dickens, Arthur G., *Reformation and Society in Sixteenth Century Europe* (New York, 1966).
  This beautifully illustrated and popularly written history is by the author of an authoritative history of the English reformation.
Elton, Geoffrey R., ed., *The Reformation, 1520–1559*, II. THE NEW CAMBRIDGE MODERN HISTORY (Cambridge, 1958).
  A distinguished reference work. The volume contains valuable chapters by E. G. Rupp and other specialists.
Elton, Geoffrey R., *Reformation Europe, 1517–1559* (Cleveland and New York, 1964).
  A brief survey.
Green, Vivian H. H., *Luther and the Reformation* (New York, 1964).
  A pleasant account with no novelties.
Grimm, Harold J., *The Reformation Era, 1500–1650*, 2nd ed. (New York, 1965).
  The most extensive treatment of the Reformation in all lands, though strongest on Germany and Lutheranism.
Hassinger, Erich, *Das Werden des neuzeitlichen Europa, 1300–1600* (Braunschweig, 1959).
  The distinguished European editor of the *Archiv für Reformationsgeschichte* stresses those aspects pointing toward modern developments, providing bibliographical data as a useful handbook.
Léonard, Émile G., *Histoire Générale du Protestantisme*, 3 vols. (Paris, 1961–64); English trans., 2 vols. (London, 1966–67).
  This general history by a leading authority on French church history,

134

well illustrated, falls into three parts: the Reformation, 1564–1700, and the decline and renewal in modern times.

Ritter, Gerhard, *Die Weltwirkung der Reformation*, 2nd ed. (Munich, 1959). This edition contains the famous essays on the sixteenth century as an historical epoch, the spiritual roots of the Reformation, Luther and the German spirit, Zwingli, Ulrich von Hutten and the Reformation, Gustav Adolf, and the like.

Thomson, Samuel Harrison, *Europe in Renaissance and Reformation* (New York, 1963). This text stresses European history at the time of the Renaissance and Reformation, rather than an organic account of the movements themselves, emphasizing eastern Europe more than is customary.

Tillmanns, Walter G., *The World and Men around Luther* (Minneapolis, 1959). The volume provides biographical vignettes on Luther's lieutenants and supporters in the broader arena.

Tüchle, Hermann, *Geschichte der Kirche*, III, *Reformation und Gegenreformation* (Einsiedeln, Zurich, Cologne, 1965). An admirably done Catholic general church history.

Reformation in Germany:

Hartung, Fritz, *Deutsche Geschichte im Zeitalter der Reformation, der Gegenreformation und des dreissigjährigen Krieges*, 2nd ed. (Berlin, 1963). By a famous political historian and excellent for political history.

Holborn, Hajo, *The Reformation*, I, *A History of Modern Germany* (New York, 1959). An excellent account by the recent president of the American Historical Association, especially impressive in political analysis.

Lau, Franz, and Bizer, Ernst, *Reformationsgeschichte Deutschlands bis 1555* (Göttingen, 1964). A fine introduction, using the latest scholarship,

Roth, Erich, *Die Reformation in Siebenbürgen. Ihr Verhältnis zu Wittenberg und der Schweiz*, 2 vols. (Graz, 1962–64). This posthumous publication describes the work of Johannes Honterus, the Swiss progress promoted by Bullinger, the Catholic advance, Klausenburger Consensus of 1557, the sacramentarian and anti-trinitarian controversies.

Skalweit, Stephan, *Reich und Reformation* (Berlin, 1967). This lively synthesis of political and cultural history treats the period between the Schmalkald War and the Peace of Augsburg more fully than is usually done and offers an impressive analysis of Ferdinand I.

Collected Essays:

Bainton, Roland H., *Studies on the Reformation* (Boston, 1963). This volume constitutes series two of Professor Bainton's *Collected Papers in Church History* and includes a section each on Luther, on the left wing of the Reformation, and on the religious struggles after the Reformation.

Blanke, Fritz, *Aus der Welt der Reformation* (Zurich, Stuttgart, 1960).
Five essays on Zwingli's judgment of himself, Calvin's comments on Zwingli, the Anabaptist Kingdom of Münster, Anabaptism, and alcoholism in the Reformation.

Bornkamm, Heinrich, *Das Jahrhundert der Reformation. Gestalten und Kräfte*, 2nd ed. (Göttingen, 1966).
Contents include a chronology of Luther's life, studies of Melanchthon, Bucer, Confessio Augustana, Copernicus in the eyes of the reformers, Maurice of Saxony, and the problem of toleration.

Gerrish, Brian, ed., *Reformers in Profile* (Philadelphia, 1967).
Ten reformers from Wycliff to Ignatius are portrayed typologically as representatives of distinctive concepts of reform.

Haikola, Lauri, *Studien zu Luther und zum Lutherthum* (Wiesbaden, 1958).
A famous Finnish scholar concentrates on theological problems.

(Lau, Franz), *450 Jahre lutherische Reformation. Festschrift für Franz Lau* (Göttingen, 1967).
This great anniversary volume contains essays by Bainton (Erasmus and Luther on the *Julius Exclusus*), Beintker, Bornkamm, Hägglund, Haikola, Loewenich, Lohse and other stars of the Reformation firmament.

Liebing, H., and Scholder, K., *Geist und Geschichte der Reformation. Festgabe Hanns Rückert* (Berlin, 1967).
This *Festschrift* in honor of the late director of the Tübingen Institute for Reformation History contains essays by Aland, Eltester, and other leading scholars.

Loewenich, Walter von, *Von Augustin zu Luther* (Witten, 1959).
The essays cover a wide range of church history subjects but the center of gravity is the Reformation.

Littel, Franklin, ed., *Reformation Studies* (Richmond, 1962).
The volume contains essays by Robert Fischer on Luther on reason, C. W. Hovland on *Anfechtung* in Luther's exegesis, John von Rohr on medieval consolation and young Luther's despair.

Pauck, Wilhelm, *The Heritage of the Reformation*, rev. ed. (Glencoe, 1961).
The most original and valuable contribution are the studies of Bucer, the third most important and irenic German reformer, in Strasburg.

Spitz, Lewis W., ed., *The Reformation—Material or Spiritual?* (Boston, 1962).
A "Problems in European Civilization" book containing selections by Bainton, Dilthey, Troeltsch, P. C. Gordon-Walker, Holborn, Erikson, Lea, Lortz and Ritter.

Vajta, Vilmos, ed., *Luther and Melanchthon* (Philadelphia, 1961).
Papers delivered at the second congress of Luther scholars, Münster, 1960.

Reformation and Scholasticism:

Dettloff, Werner, *Die Entwicklung der Akzeptations- und Verdienstlehre von Duns Scotus bis Luther unter Berücksichtigung der Franziskanertheologen* (Münster, 1963).
This study traces Luther's inheritance of the *acceptatio divina* from Duns

Scotus via Occam and Gabriel Biel, whom Dettloff evaluates very low.

Grane, Leif, *Contra Gabrielem: Luthers Auseinandersetzung mit Gabriel Biel in der Disputatio contra scholasticam theologiam 1517* (Copenhagen, 1962).

The Copenhagen church historian provides a summary of Biel's theology, a detailed commentary on the disputation, and an analysis of the doctrinal matters on which Luther differed and which he developed independently.

Hennig, Gerhard, *Cajetan und Luther: ein historischer Beitrag zur Begegnung von Thomismus und Reformation* (Stuttgart, 1966).

In Cajetan Luther encountered the leading Thomist of his day, but Cajetan represented a rigidified and formalized Thomism.

Oberman, Heiko, *Forerunners of the Reformation* (New York), 1966).

The director of the Institute for Reformation History, Tübingen, offers key texts from scholastic, humanist, and moralistic reformers together with an essay on reformers before the Reformation.

Oberman, Heiko, *The Harvest of Medieval Theology: Gabriel Biel and Late Medieval Nominalism* (Cambridge, Mass., 1963).

In this first volume of a trilogy the author argues for the vigor of late scholasticism, holds Biel to be on a high plane with Occam on philosophical, but especially theological, issues, transmitting an "impressively coherent structure" of Occam's system to Luther.

Oberman, Heiko, and Courtenay, William, eds., *Gabrielis Biel canonis missae expositio*, I-III (Wiesbaden, 1963-66).

A scholarly edition of a key text.

Pfürtner, Stephanus, *Luther und Thomas in Gespräch* (Heidelberg, 1961).

This comparison of Luther and Thomas' view of the certainty of salvation moves on to criticize the decree on justification of the Council of Trent as inadequately expressing the richer teaching of Thomas.

Scharleman, Robert P., *Thomas Aquinas and John Gerhard* (New Haven, 1964).

A comparison of the great thirteenth-century scholastic and the Lutheran dogmatician reveals a certain dynamism of the Word in the evangelical theologian not so evident in Thomas.

Schwarz, Reinhold, *Fides, Spes, und Caritas beim jungen Luther unter besonderer Berücksichtigung der mittelalterlichen Tradition* (Berlin, 1962).

Luther's exegetical commentaries from the *Dictata super Psalterium* to Galatians reveal that he consistently denied to *caritas* and the other theological virtues an independent habitual quality, defining grace as a benignity of God, not as a *habitus* in man.

Vorster, Hans, *Das Freiheitsverständnis bei Thomas von Aquin und Martin Luther* (Göttingen, 1965).

An irenic rereading of Thomas and Luther, finding Thomas closer to Luther, behind a different vocabulary, and further from the definitions of Trent, although still pointing out sharp contrasts between Thomas and Luther.

Reformation and Humanism:

Andreas, Willy, *Deutschland vor der Reformation*, 6th ed. (Stuttgart, 1959).

The Heidelberg historian's classical survey of political, ecclesiastical, and cultural circumstances on the eve of the Reformation.

Bonorand, Conradin, *Vadians Weg vom Humanismus zur Reformation und seine Vorträge über die Apostelgeschichte (1523)* (St. Gallen, 1962).
The impact of the Scriptures upon Vadian, who had been prominent in Vienna as a humanist, is emphasized.

Dufour, Alain, "Humanisme et réformation," *Rapports III Commissions. Comité International des sciences Historiques, XIIe Congrès International des Sciences Historiques*, 57–74.
The Genevan scholar discusses the status of the question and supplies essential bibliography.

Garside, Charles, *Zwingli and the Arts* (New Haven, 1966).
A study of Zwingli's attitude toward and effect upon music and the visual arts.

Kirchner, Hubert, *Johannes Sylvius Egranus. Ein Beitrag zum Verhältnis von Reformation und Humanismus* (Berlin, 1961).
This biographical study of a minor figure illustrates concretely intellectual forces operative on a broad scale.

Nauert, Charles, *Agrippa and the Crisis of Renaissance Thought* (Urbana, 1965).
The author seeks to resolve the paradox of Agrippa's occultism and skepticism, fideism and critical rationalism.

Newald, Richard, *Problemen und Gestalten des deutschen Humanismus* (Berlin, 1963).
A collection of portraits of such humanists and reformers as Erasmus, Celtis, Hutten, Johann Müller, Geiler von Kaisersberg, Wimpfeling, Brant, Murner, and Ringmann.

Oelrich, K. H., *Der späte Erasmus und die Reformation* (Münster, 1961).
Erasmus is depicted as essentially a good Catholic and more conservative in his last years than is usually supposed.

Rogge, Joachim, *Zwingli und Erasmus. Die Friedensgedanken des jungen Zwingli* (Stuttgart, 1962).
The influence of Erasmian spiritualism on the young Zwingli is explored in terms of their peace-mindedness.

Seidlmayer, Michael, *Wege und Wandlungen des Humanismus* (Göttingen, 1965).
Long concerned with problems such as the religious thought of Italian humanists, the author here offers studies of Cusanus, Celtis, Hutten, Dante's imperial conception, and the idea of Rome in the Middle Ages.

Spitz, Lewis W., *The Religious Renaissance of the German Humanists* (Cambridge, Mass., 1963).
This study of the religious thought of the humanists from Agricola to Erasmus uses Luther as the *terminus ad quem*, indicating his positive cultural relation to, but theological differences from, humanism.

The Posting of the Ninety-Five Theses: (In order of appearance.)

Volz, Hans, *Martin Luthers Thesenanschlag und dessen Vorgeschichte* (Weimar, 1959).

Volz argued that the nailing episode took place on the morning of November 1.

Iserloh, Erwin, "Luthers Thesenanschlag: Tatsache oder Legende?" *Trierer Theologische Zeitschrift*, 70 (1961), 303–12; reprinted (Wiesbaden, 1962).

Iserloh, ecumenically motivated, held that Luther did not post them at all but merely submitted his theses obediently to the episcopal superiors.

Lohse, Bernard, "Der Stand der Debatte über Luthers Thesenanschlag," *Luther*, 34 (1963), 132–36.

A report on the course of the new voluminous debates.

Steitz, H., "Luthers 95 Thesen: Stationen eines Gelehrtenstreites," *Jahrbuch der hessischen kirchengeschichtlichen Vereinigung*, 14 (1963), 179–91.

Aland, Kurt, "Der Thesenanschlag fand—und zwar am 31. Oktober 1517— statt," *Geschichte in Wissenschaft und Unterricht*, 16 (1965), 686–94.

This essay, enlarged, was published in English as *Martin Luther's 95 Theses* (St. Louis, 1967).

Iserloh, Erwin, *Luther zwischen Reform und Reformation. Der Thesenanschlag fand nicht statt* (Münster, 1966).

After an initial sketch of the history of indulgences, an argument *a silentio* from the absence of references to the nailing in the sources, the book grants that the Reformation still began on Oct. 31, 1517.

Honselmann, Clemens, *Urfassung und Drucke der Ablassthesen Martin Luthers und ihre Veröffentlichung* (Paderborn, 1966).

The dubious argument is developed that Luther prepared two versions of the theses, one sent to the bishop and archbishop and another with the preamble for publication in reaction to Tetzel's anti-theses.

Lau, Franz, "Die gegenwärtige Diskussion um Luthers Thesenanschlag," *Luther-Jahrbuch* (1967), 11–59.

The Leipzig church historian recounts the debate, and favors the older tradition.

Bornkamm, Heinrich, "Thesen und Thesenanschlag Luthers. Zur Frage des 31. Oktober 1517," *Geist und Geschichte der Reformation* (Berlin, 1966), 179–218 (*Sonderabdruck*, 1967).

The Heidelberg historian argues that the 95 theses were genuine disputation theses falling into the series of Wittenberg disputations, 1516–18, that they belonged to the proper sphere of a professor's activities and were therefore no affront to Luther's ecclesiastical superiors.

Schwiebert, Ernest G., "The Theses and Wittenberg," *Luther for an Ecumenical Age*, Carl S. Meyer, ed. (St. Louis, 1967), 120–43.

The theses are placed in the university setting and Wittenberg University practice.

Luther's Development:

Aland, Kurt, *Der Weg zur Reformation: Zeitpunkt und Charakter des reformatorischen Erlebnisses Martin Luthers* (Munich, 1965).

A late date for the "tower experience" is favored, between February 15 and March 28, 1518.

Erikson, Erik H., *Young Man Luther* (New York, 1958).
> An attempt to use Luther as a case study in exploring the utility of psychoanalysis for history.

Kantzenbach, Friedrich Wilhelm, *Martin Luther und die Anfänge der Reformation* (Gütersloh, 1965).
> Though a brief account of Luther's development, this work takes into account current problems in Luther research and analysis. A sequel volume, *Die Reformation in Deutschland und Europa*, same place and date, sketches the period from the Diet of Augsburg 1530, through the dogmatic controversies.

Müller-Streisand, Rosemarie, *Luthers Weg von der Reformation zur Restauration* (Halle [Saale], 1964).
> An attempt to trace the lines of development and discontinuity in Luther's church-critical theology and the basis for change. Necessarily sketchy.

Luther's Theology:

Althaus, Paul, *Die Theologie Martin Luthers* (Gütersloh, 1962; English tr., Philadelphia, 1967).
> The distinguished theologian invests a life-time of study in a statement of Luther's whole theology.

Asendorf, Ulrich, *Eschatologie bei Luther* (Göttingen, 1967).

Barth, Hans-Martin, *Der Teufel und Jesus Christus in der Theologie Martin Luthers* (Göttingen, 1967).
> This study in seeing the dynamic of Luther's concept of the cosmic struggle is superior to Martin Rade's earlier work on the subject.

Barth, Karl, *Der Götze Wackelt!* (Berlin, 1961).
> This volume by the main founder of neo-orthodoxy republishes the famous essay, pp. 71–86, "Die Reformation als Entscheidung," arguing for the essentially theological concerns of the reformers.

Brandenburg, Albert, *Gericht und Evangelium: Zur Worttheologie in Luthers erster Psalmenvorlesung* (Paderborn, 1960).
> A surprising, highly existential interpretation of Luther's theology based on the *Dictata* by a Catholic scholar.

Bizer, Ernst, *Fides ex auditu. Eine Untersuchung über die Entdeckung der Gerechtigkeit Gottes durch Martin Luther*, 2nd ed. (Neukirchen, 1961).
> The author takes seriously Luther's 1545 witness to the time of the "tower experience" as at the time of the indulgences controversy and beginning of the second series of lectures on the Psalms, or 1518. He associates it with the application of Rom. 1:17 in answer to Cajetan and stresses the Word by whom God justifies men.

Ebeling, Gerhard, *Luther: Einführung in sein Denken* (Tübingen, 1964).
> The author of a monumental study of Luther's exegesis (*Evangelische Evangelienauslegung*) here seeks to penetrate to the core of Luther's theology, to the *verbum incarnatum*, and stresses the existential and humanly most urgent components of Luther's thought.

Gerrish, Brian, *Grace and Reason* (Oxford, 1962).

    The question of Luther's rationalism and fideism is brilliantly discussed in terms of Luther's threefold use of the term reason as natural, arrogant, and regenerate reason.

Hermann, Rudolph, *Gesammelte Studien zur Theologie Luthers und der Reformation* (Göttingen, 1960).

    An omnibus volume of a long-time Luther scholar's essays including his famous study of the figure of Samson as a wonderman of Old Testament history.

Hermann, Rudolph, *Luthers Theologie*, I (Göttingen, 1967).

    Luther studies from the posthumous papers and periodical publications of a well known Reformation scholar.

Joest, Wilfried, *Ontologie der Person bei Luther* (Göttingen, 1967).

    The author of an earlier volume on the third use of the law here, while conceding that Luther was not metaphysically a high ontologist, argues that he operated with ontological conceptions in theology and was not a thorough existentialist.

Kadai, Heino O., *Accents in Luther's Theology* (St. Louis, 1967).

    This 450th anniversary commemorative volume contains essays on key theological conceptions by Hermann Sasse, Ernest Koenker, Jaroslav Pelikan, Martin Marty and other scholars.

Löfgren, David, *Die Theologie der Schöpfung bei Luther* (Göttingen, 1960).

    Luther understood creation as a continuing process whenever God acts through His powerful Word.

Modalsi, Ole, *Das Gericht nach den Werken* (Göttingen, 1963).

    Luther ascribed a declarative significance to good works, which serve as proofs of the inner, living, saving faith.

Nilsson, Kjell Ove, *Simul: Das Miteinander von Göttlichem und Menschlichem in Luthers Theologie* (Göttingen, 1966).

    Emphasizing Luther's stress upon the immanence of God in creation and in the church, this study explores the coexistence of God and man in the realms of nature and grace.

Peters, Albrecht, *Glaube und Werk: Luthers Rechtfertigungslehre im Lichte der Heiligen Schrift* (Berlin, 1962).

    The author emphasizes the fusion of faith and good works in the total life of the Christian.

Pinomaa, Lennart, *Sieg des Glaubens* (Göttingen, 1964); Engl. tr., *Faith Victorious* (Philadelphia, 1963).

    The great Finnish Luther scholar, author of an earlier existential interpretation of Luther, stresses lively faith as the *vita cordis*.

Robinson, William Childs, *The Reformation: A Rediscovery of Grace* (Grand Rapids, Mich., 1962).

    A positive evangelical restatement of the centrality of the *sola gratia*.

Schloemann, Martin, *Natürliches und gepredigtes Gesetz bei Luther* (Berlin, 1961).

    Paying special attention to the controversy with the antinomians, the author explores the question of the unity of Luther's conception of law.

Seils, Martin, *Der Gedanke vom Zusammenwirken Gottes und des Menschen in Luthers Theologie* (Gütersloh, 1962).
"Good works within us but not without us," reads one of Luther's favorite phrases. This study of *cooperatio* between God and man develops the thought of the Christian life as a *negotium cum Deo*.

Stockmann, Robert, *Der königliche Weg* (Mainz, 1965).
A young Lutheran clergyman studies Luther's understanding of the way of salvation in his exegesis of Romans.

The Word, Scripture, and Tradition:

Beiser, Friedrich, *Claritas scripturae bei Martin Luther* (Göttingen, 1966).
The question of the perspicuity of Scripture, controverted in the debate with Erasmus, the basis for the hermeneutical principle *Scriptura scriptura interpretatur*, and related problems are involved in this study.

Bornkamm, Karin, *Luthers Auslegungen des Galaterbriefs von 1519 und 1531* (Berlin, 1963).
The comparison of the two commentaries reveals the completeness of Luther's evangelical-theological development in the first and deviation on only minor points in the second.

Grundmann, Walter, *Der Römerbrief des Apostels Paulus und seine Auslegung durch Martin Luther* (Weimar, 1964).
The author studies the position of Paul and Luther in and on Romans and finds in Paul an apocalyptic—Kairos—element not found in Luther, who used justification against the views of fellow Christians, not Jews, gnostics, or pagans.

Kooiman, Willem Jan, *Luther and the Bible* (Philadelphia, 1961).
The Dutch minister-scholar stresses the centrality of the Scriptures as authority; a popular but learned work.

Krause, Gerhard, *Studien zu Luthers Auslegung der kleinen Propheten* (Tübingen, 1962).
The analysis goes beyond philology to compare traditional and novel elements in Luther's treatment of the minor prophets.

Pelikan, Jaroslav, *Luther the Expositor* (St. Louis, 1959).
The Titus Street Professor of Ecclesiastical History at Yale and editor of the American Edition of *Luther's Works* analyzes Luther's exegetical principles and presents case studies of their application.

Sandstrom, Peter G., *Luther's Sense of Himself as an Interpreter of the Word to the World* (Amherst, Mass., 1961).
A precocious senior-honors thesis, the essay describes Luther's breakthrough to confidence in the power of the spoken Word.

Wernle, Hams, *Allegorie und Erlebnis bei Luther* (Bern, 1960).
Luther's fighting nature led him to challenge traditional allegorical interpretations and his experience produced impatience with dreamlike imprecise readings of a text, yet this man destined for modernity was a creature of his times who resorted to allegory and the views of the collective tradition.

Wölfel, Eberhard, *Luther und die Skepsis. Eine Studie zur Kohelet-Exegese* (Munich, 1958).

Luther saw the vanity of life not in things outside of man but in the void within man which only faith can overcome.

Church and Sacraments:

Asheim, Ivar, ed., *Kirche, Mystik, Heiligung und das Natürliche bei Luther* (Göttingen, 1967).

The volume contains the papers of the 1966 Luther Congress in Helsinki.

Bizer, Ernst, *Luther und der Papst* (Munich, 1958).

The author of the widely discussed book *Fides ex auditu* here argues that it was his discovery of Romans 1:17 that drove Luther into opposition to the papacy.

Headley, John M., *Luther's View of Church History* (New Haven, 1963).

Luther had not a humanist or simply an Augustinian view of church history, but a distinctively Biblical understanding.

Höhne, Wolfgang, *Luthers Anschauung über die Kontinuität der Kirche* (Berlin, 1964).

Luther thought of the church, never the churches, as the *una sancta*.

Johns, Christa Tecklenburg, *Luthers Konzilsidee in ihrer historischen Bedingtheit und ihrem reformatorischen Neuansatz* (Berlin, 1966).

This young evangelical scholar traces the development of Luther's conciliar thought and contrasts his new conception of the church and council to that of the traditional Catholic understanding of council.

Köhler, Erika, *Martin Luther und der Festbrauch* (Cologne, 1959).

Lieberg, Hellmut, *Amt und Ordination bei Luther und Melanchthon* (Göttingen, 1962).

This comprehensive monograph emphasizes the call to the office, divine character of the office, the importance of ordination, and the derivation of the office from the universal priesthood of all believers.

Sasse, Hermann, *This Is My Body. Luther's Contention for the Real Presence in the Sacrament of the Altar* (Minneapolis, 1959).

The conservative Lutheran theologian examines Luther's views against the traditional background, compares them with those of Zwingli, and draws conclusions for the church today.

Ethics:

Althaus, Paul, *Die Ethik Martin Luthers* (Gütersloh, 1965).

The Christian is seen as a citizen of two very different kingdoms, that of God and that of the world, and his ethical life is lived in a state of tension, product of the eschatological expectation.

Cranz, Ferdinand Edward, *An Essay on the Development of Luther's Thought on Justice, Law and Society* (Cambridge, Mass., 1959).

An outstanding study which depicts 1518–19 as a crucial turning point for Luther in reorienting his social thought, tracing his development in the concept of calling, of the two governments of God corresponding to

Christian righteousness and civil justice, and of the three hierarchies of church, household, and polity, all equally holy.

Esnault, René H., *Luther et le monachisme aujourd'hui* (Geneva, 1964).
The author examines the *De votis monasticis* and raises questions about the religious life addressed to the circumstances of our times.

Lazareth, William H., *Luther on the Christian Home: An Application of the Social Ethics of the Reformation* (Philadelphia, 1960).
A thorough study of "marriage as a Christian calling" against the background of Luther's teachings on the Christian's righteousness and social justice.

Lohse, Bernhard, *Mönchtum und Reformation: Luthers Auseinandersetzung mit dem Mönchsideal des Mittelalters* (Göttingen, 1963).
The monograph proceeds from a study of Luther's *De votis monasticis* to a review of the general principles upon which he based his opposition to monasticism.

Wolf, Ernst, *Peregrinatio* I (Munich, 1962); II (1965).
Whereas the first volume of essays has to do more with theological and ecclesiological problems, the second deals with problems of church law and social ethics.

Ziemke, Donald, *Love for the Neighbor in Luther's Theology* (Minneapolis, 1963).
Luther emphasized the pre-eminence of love over legalism.

Society and the State:

Chrisman, Miriam, *Strasbourg and the Reform* (New Haven, 1967).
This study of the institutional and intellectual transformation of a key city, 1523–1533, is a model of yet further work needed on other imperial cities.

Huegli, Albert, ed., *Church and State under God* (St. Louis, 1964).
This volume contains an extensive essay on the impact of the Reformation on church-state issues.

Lutz, Heinrich, *Ragione di stato und christliche Staatsethik im 16. Jahrhundert* (Münster, 1961).
The Vienna Peutinger scholar turns his attention here to questions of Machiavellism, Christian humanist and reformers' theories of the state, presenting in brief statement the theories of Pontano, Machiavelli, Pole, Francis di Vitoria, Gentillet, and Botero.

Moeller, Bernd, *Reichsstadt und Reformation* (Gütersloh, 1962).
The special role of the city-state, the city councils, the proprietary church is spelled out in this slender but not slight volume. In a work on *Zürich und die Reformation in Konstanz* (Gütersloh, 1961), Moeller provides a fascinating case study, though it should have been researched in greater detail.

Strauss, Gerald, *Nuremberg in the 16th Century* (New York, 1966).
Like E. W. Monter, *Calvin's Geneva* (New York, 1967), this volume seeks to place the religious, educational, and cultural transformation within the socio-political setting of the city-state, though with some odd theories

about the Protestant stress on sin and the bourgeois psyche.

Swanson, Guy E., *Religion and Regime, A Sociological Account of the Reformation* (Ann Arbor, 1967).

A weird attempt, based upon several false premises, to relate the disbelief in God's immanence in Protestant lands (sic!) to their prior political experience and Catholic belief in immanence to a political tradition of strong central government pervading all aspects of life; a parade of historical errors gotten up in fine social-scientific costuming. His suggestion that guilt feelings motivated the business mentality to accept Protestantism is untenable on various grounds, not the least of which was the acceptance of Protestantism in many lands by all classes, rendering such speculation idle.

Education and Culture:

Arndt, E., *Luthers deutsches Sprachschaffen* (Berlin, 1962).

Familiar comments on Luther's contribution to the development of the German language.

Asheim, Ivar, *Glaube und Erziehung bei Luther* (Heidelberg, 1961).

The attempt is less to portray Luther as pedagogical theorist than to show how he approached education as a theologian.

Bluhm, M. L., *Martin Luther: Creative Translator* (St. Louis, 1965).

A skilled German philologist examines Luther's work as a Biblical translator and creator of the German Bible and therewith of the new High German.

Bornkamm, Heinrich, *Luther als Schriftsteller* (Heidelberg, 1965).

A brief study.

Dillenberger, John, *Protestant Thought and Natural Science* (Garden City, New York, 1960).

A brilliant study of the dominance of Aristotle and the three stages in the resistance to and final reception of the Copernican theories.

Loewenich, Walter von, *Luther und der Neuprotestantismus* (Witten, 1963).

The great Erlangen student of Luther's *theologia crucis* examines the way in which modern theologians have viewed Luther and Luther's influence in turn upon existentialism, crisis theology and neo-orthodox modes in modern theology.

McLelland, Joseph, *The Reformation and its Significance Today* (Philadelphia, 1962).

The author defines a reformed Church as one that follows the spirit of the 16th century in carrying on the work of reform, not one that is content to sing the reformers' praises for what they once did. In a popular style he sketches representative reformers and then stresses the need for a historic perspective for present-day liturgy.

Martin Luther Lectures (Decorah, Iowa, 1957–61).

I. Luther Today (1957).

II. More About Luther (1958).

III. The Mature Luther (1959).

IV. Luther and Culture (1960).

V. Luther and the Twentieth Century (1961).

An aggregation of Luther scholars such as Bainton, Grimm, Tappert, and E. Gordon Rupp offers lectures on subjects as widely diverse as Luther's role as a professor to Luther in America.

Wünsch, Georg, *Luther und die Gegenwart* (Stuttgart, 1961).

A work which seeks to relate Luther's thought in a positive as well as a negative way to twentieth-century thought and society, to Marx, the anthropological realists, existentialists, and the like.

Ecumenical Reappraisals:

Asmussen, Hans, *et alii*, *The Unfinished Reformation* (Notre Dame, 1961).

The Lutheran opponent of the Nazis here, with others, argues the need for a continuing reformation leading to unity in Christendom.

Aulen, Gustav, *Reformation and Catholicity* (Philadelphia, 1961).

The Swedish Lutheran's work now translated into English stresses the evangelical concern for the *una sancta*.

Beyna, Werner, *Das moderne katholische Lutherbild*, VII, *Koinonia: Beiträge zur ökumenischen Spiritualität und Theologie*, Thomas Sartory, ed. (Essen, 1967).

A fuller survey than was up to now available on the impact of ecumenical and irenic Catholic scholars upon the interpretation of the Reformation.

Dolan, John, *History of the Reformation. A Conciliatory Assessment of Opposite Views* (New York, 1965).

This volume by a former Notre Dame professor now at South Carolina University is less a history of the Reformation than it is a collection of studies of the historiographic controversies, the failings of the medieval church, the aborted reform efforts of Gerson and Cusanus, and the reassertion of papal power in the Catholic Reformation.

Düfel, Hans, *Luthers Stellung zur Marienverehrung* (Göttingen, 1967).

The high regard of the reformers for the Virgin Mary is a theme now being developed in an ecumenical way, for Luther kept an icon of Mary in his study throughout his life. Two interesting text editions in this connection are:

Martin Luther, *Le Magnificat*, pref. du Cardinal Martin et de Roger Schutz, prieur de Taizé (Collection: Approches oecumeniques) (Mulhouse, 1967).

Tappolet, Walter, ed., *Das Marienlob der Reformatoren. Luther. Calvin. Zwingli. Bullinger.* (Tübingen, 1962).

Ebneter, Albert, s.j., *Luther und das Konzil* (Vienna, 1962).

Ebneter, in contrast to the Protestant Kolde in 1876, who wrote that Luther's break with the church was marked less by his rejection of the papacy than of the council, shows in outline what Luther hoped for from a council. A reprint of the *Zeitschrift für katholische Theologie* 84 (1962), 1–48, article.

Edel, Gottfried, *Das gemeinkatholische mittelalterliche Erbe beim iungen Luther* (Marburg, 1962).

An irenic evangelical scholar in this Mainz dissertation accentuates the universal, truly catholic elements in young Luther's thought.

Fraenkel, Pierre, *Einigungsbestrebungen in der Reformationszeit* (Wiesbaden, 1965). The noted Swiss Melanchthon scholar, author of a work on Melanchthon's knowledge and use of patristic literature, in this address given at the Institute for European History in Mainz pays tribute to the 16th-century efforts to restore the unity of the church.

Hacker, Paul, *Das Ich im Glauben bei Martin Luther* (Graz, 1966). A Catholic scholar wrestles earnestly with Luther about the central question of the truth of the Gospel. He criticizes Luther sharply for his pre-Descartes Cartesianism (*credo ergo sum*) and operative principle of correlating antithetical propositions. Very basic but honest criticism.

Hirsch, Emanuel, *Das Wesen des reformatorischen Christentums* (Berlin, 1963). The author of the massive five-volume history of modern evangelical theology here assesses the essential religious good inherited by modern Protestantism, without wishing to repristinate old forms, and examines such questions as evangelical freedom and papal power.

Iserloh, Erwin, and Manns, Peter, *Festgabe Joseph Lortz*, 2 vols. (Baden-Baden, 1957–58). The two massive volumes with some forty contributors, Evangelical and Catholic scholars, cover widespread subjects on the Reformation, faith, and history.

Iserloh, E., and Repgen, Karl, eds., *Reformata reformanda* (*Festgabe für Hubert Jedin*), I (Münster, 1965). This volume honoring the great authority on the Council of Trent contains essays by Lortz on Luther's spiritual posture, by Peter Manns on Luther's doctrine of justification in the large Galatians commentary, and the like.

Karrer, Otto, *Das Erbe der Reformation in katholischer Sicht. Studien zur ökumenischen Begegnung mit dem Protestantismus* (Vienna, 1963). A Catholic scholar, expert on the Second Vatican Council, reflects on the significance of the Reformation today for ecumenical dialogue.

Lackmann, Max, *The Augsburg Confession and Catholic Unity* (New York, 1963). A Lutheran pastor in lectures to Catholic audiences seeks to demonstrate "how the *Confessio Augustana* draws separated Christians into an intensive movement toward each other."

Lortz, Joseph, *Die Reformation in Deutschland*, 2 vols., 4th ed. (Freiburg, 1962). The pioneer Catholic revisionist in this new edition maintains his view of Luther as a *homo religiosus*, an earnest reformer who was more sincere than Erasmus, but too subjective and unable to subordinate himself to ecclesiastical authority. This work is being translated into English.

Two of Lortz's minor works have been published in English, Daniel O'Hanlon, s.j., ed., *How the Reformation Came* (New York, 1964); John C. Dwyer, s.j., ed., *The Reformation. A Problem for Today* (Westminster, Maryland, 1964).

McDonough, Thomas, *The Law and the Gospel in Luther: A Study of Martin Luther's Confessional Writings* (Oxford, 1963).

The Dominican scholar reveals the influence of Lortz's ecumenism, but his treatment of the tension between law and gospel, doubt and faith in Luther's theology falls short of doing Luther full justice. He seeks to establish three points, namely that according to Luther man remains his whole life as a sinner under the wrath of God, that in justification by faith man is purely passive, and that justification is entirely forensic and imputative.

McNeill, John T., *Unitive Protestantism: The Ecumenical Spirit and its Persistent Expression* (Richmond, 1964).

The noted Calvin scholar offers a revised edition of his pioneer work of 1930.

McSorley, Harry J., *Luthers Lehre vom unfreien Willen nach seiner Hauptschrift "De servo arbitrio" im Lichte der biblischen Tradition* (Munich, 1966).

This work by an American Catholic scholar is the first in an ecumenical series edited by Heinrich Fries. The second volume will be on the theme of "Luthers Lehre von der Rechtfertigung im Spiegel katholischer Manualien."

Meinhold, Peter, *Luther heute* (Berlin, 1967).

The Kiel University ecumenical Lutheran stresses the importance of Luther's reforming activity for ecumenism today.

Meyer, Carl S., ed., *Luther for an Ecumenical Age* (St. Louis, 1967).

This 450th anniversary volume contains essays by E. Gordon Rupp on the theology of the cross, Harold Grimm on Spengler and the Nuremberg Council, Norman Nagel on *Sacramentum et exemplum*, Pelikan on infant baptism, and other leading scholars.

Meyer, Hans Bernhard, *Luther und die heilige Messe* (Paderborn, 1965).

The able Ingolstadt Catholic theologian finds that many of Vatican II's reforms were advocated by Luther and is concerned with compromise formulas on the Sacrament as sacrifice and other controverted questions.

Pelikan, Jaroslav, *Obedient Rebels: Catholic Substance and Protestant Principle in Luther's Reformation* (New York, 1964).

The ecumenical Lutheran professor of church history at Yale explores the paradox that Luther was more "catholic" than many of his opponents, was Catholic in substance, Protestant in principle, and only reluctantly was forced out of the institutional unity of the church.

Pfeilschifter, Georg, ed., *Acta reformationis Catholicae ecclesiam Germaniae concernentia saeculi XVI. Die Reformverhandlungen des deutschen Episkopats von 1520 bis 1570* (Regensburg, 1959).

The reform efforts of the church in the 16th century provide an important facet for scholarly exploration with significant ecumenical implications.

Todd, John, *Martin Luther* (Westminster, Maryland, 1964).

This biography by an English Catholic layman, an admirer of the Methodist Luther scholar E. Gordon Rupp, goes beyond the rehabilitation of Luther's person and character to an appreciation of the deep religious concerns of the reformer.

Zeeden, Ernst Walter, *Katholische Überlieferung in den lutherischen Kirchenordnungen des 16. Jahrhunderts* (Münster, 1959).

The irenic Catholic reformation scholar describes the church's heritage of the pre-Reformation days incorporated into the Lutheran church order, in the order of worship services, liturgical practices, sacramental customs, the church year, processions, and other usages.

Zeeden, Ernst Walter, *Martin Luther, Johannes Calvin und zeitgenössische katholische Stimmen zur Reformation* (Düsseldorf, 1959).

Brief excerpts from Luther, Calvin, and such Catholics as Contarini and Berthold von Chiemsee giving their views of the Reformation.

Marxist Interpretation of the Reformation: (No comment.)

Bensing, M., "Friedrich Engels' Schrift über den deutschen Bauernkrieg—ihre aktuelle Bedeutung 1850 und ihre Rolle bei der Herausbildung der marxistischen Geschichtswissenschaft," *Friedrich Engels' Kampf und Vermächtnis* (Berlin, 1961), pp. 158 ff.

Bensing, M., *Thomas Müntzer und der Thüringer Aufstand 1525* (Berlin, 1966).

Bensing, M., and Hoyer, S., *Der deutsche Bauernkrieg, 1524–1526* (Berlin, 1965).

Brendler, G., *Das Täuferreich zu Münster 1534-1535* (Berlin, 1966).

Fabiunke, Günter, *Martin Luther als Nationalökonom* (Berlin, 1963).

Friesen, Abraham, *The Marxist Interpretation of the Reformation* (diss., Stanford University, 1967).

Koch, Hans-Gerhard, *Luthers Reformation in kommunistischer Sicht* (Stuttgart, 1967).

Macek, J., *Der tiroler Bauernkrieg und Michael Gaismair* (Berlin, 1965).

Paterna, E., *Da stunden die Bergkleute auff! Die Klassenkämpfe der mansfeldischen Bergarbeiter im 16. u. 17. Jahrhundert und ihre ökonomischen und sozialen Ursachen* (Berlin, 1960).

Steinmetz, M., *Deutschland von 1476 bis 1648, Lehrbuch der deutschen Geschichte,* III (Berlin, 1965).

Stern, Leo, *Philipp Melanchthon, Humanist, Reformator, Praeceptor Germaniae* (Berlin, 1963).

Zschäbitz, Gerhard, *Martin Luther. Grösse und Grenze,* I (Berlin, 1967).

Zschäbitz, G., *Zur mitteldeutschen Wiedertäuferbewegung nach dem grossen Bauernkrieg* (Berlin, 1958).

Luther and Other Traditions:

Doernberg, Erwin, *Henry VIII and Luther* (Stanford, 1961).

Replete with selections from their robust personal exchanges.

Oyer, J. S., *Lutheran Reformers Against Anabaptists* (The Hague, 1965).

Tjernagel, Neelak S., *Henry VIII and the Lutherans* (St. Louis, 1966).

The emphasis is upon Lutheran influence in England, a view opposed by scholars such as Leonard Trinterud, who would allow a larger than usual influence to Zurich.

Bibliographical Aids and Editions:

Benzing, Joseph, *Lutherbibliographie, Verzeichnis der gedruckten Schriften Martin Luthers bis zu dessen Tod (1546)*, 3 vols. (Baden-Baden, 1965–66).
Bibliographie de la Réforme 1450–1648: Ouvrages parus de 1940 à 1955, 2nd ed. (Leiden, 1961).
Delumeau, Jean, *Naissance et affirmation de la Réforme* (Paris, 1965).
Eberhardt, Hans, and Schlechte, Horst, eds., *Die Reformation in Dokumenten* (Weimar, 1967).
Grimm, Harold J., *The Reformation in Recent Historical Thought* (New York, 1964).
Hillerbrand, Hans, *The Reformation. A Narrative History. Related by Contemporary Observers and Participants* (New York, 1964).
Index Aurelianus. Catalogus librorum sedecimo saeculo impressorum, 5 vols. (Baden-Baden, 1962–1964).
    A complete short-title catalogue of all printed books of the sixteenth century.
Lehmann, Helmuth, and Pelikan, Jaroslav, general eds., *Luther's Works*, American Edition, 56 vols. (St. Louis and Philadelphia, 1955—).
"Luther Research since 1945," *Lutheran World*, 13 (1966), no. 3.
    Contains reports by Friedrich Kantzenbach, Regin Prenter, Lauri Haikola, Carter Lindberg, and Otto Pesch.
Spitz, Lewis W., "Current Accents in Luther Study: 1960–67," *Theological Studies*, XXVIII, no. 3 (Sept., 1967), 549–573.
Spitz, Lewis W., "The Lutheran Reformation in American Historiography," *The Maturing of American Lutheranism*, Benjamin Johnson and Herbert Neve, eds. (Minneapolis, 1968), part 2.
Spitz, Lewis W., and Kadai, Heino, *Guide to Reformation Literature* (St. Louis, 1967).
Spitz, Lewis W., ed., *The Protestant Reformation* (Englewood Cliffs, N.J., 1966).
Stupperich, Robert, "Lutherforschung und Reformationsgeschichte," *Archiv für Kulturgeschichte*, 43 (1961), 377–92.
Vajta, Vilmos, ed., *Lutherforschung heute* (Berlin, 1958).

"Every great book is an action,
    just as every great action is a book!"
MARTIN LUTHER